(2020) raised $45,000 USD for Help for Heroes, which supports UK veterans and servicemembers; and Project Valor (2017) saw WoWS, WoT, and WoWP collectively raise $75,000 USD for a veteran housing program. Preserving historical ship museums: *World of Warships*, in partnership with museums across the world to support the preservation of naval history and the education of the global community, raised $50,000 USD for the restoration of USS *Batfish* (2019) and $400,000 USD for the restoration of USS *Texas* (2017). Finally, supporting the local community: a 24-hour charity livestream (2019) raised $43,000 USD for the Save the Children organization, and also raised $78,000 USD for Team Rubicon and the victims of Hurricane Harvey in 2017.

The United States Naval Institute (USNI) has been a proud partner of *World of Warships* and Wargaming since December 2019. Wargaming has a made a commitment to naval history through various programs and events over the past years. It produces excellent video content with its *Naval Legends* series on YouTube, and hosts events on board museum ships where members of the gaming and naval history communities can get together and experience living history in person. *World of Warships* and Wargaming are also great sponsors of the Historic Naval Ships Association (HNSA). USNI thanks Wargaming and *World of Warships* for their continued support of the naval history community and their participation in this Naval History Special Edition. Please see the back cover for a special offer for *World of Warships* PC and *World of Warships: Legends*.

In 1940, during the war, the United States began looking for a replacement for the obsolete and weak Browning AA machine guns. The 20-mm automatic Oerlikon, significantly improved by that time, proved to be very useful. In 1941, production began in the United States, and soon the Oerlikons were mounted on almost every warship, from boats to battleships. USS *Massachusetts* carried 35 of these weapons during World War II.

The Mark 12 5-inch/38-cal gun would prove invaluable to the U.S. Navy in World War II. The MK 29 and 32 dual-purpose mounts were a highly efficient artillery system. A heavy-duty power drive and reliable mechanism ensured a fast horizontal and vertical aiming speed—perfect for use in the antiaircraft role. The mount had a nominal rate of fire of 15 shots per minute, but that could be increased for a short period of time, shooting up to 22 shells per minute. Each 5/38 shell weighed more than 50 lbs. USS *Massachusetts* was built with 10 MK 32 mounts, 5 per side.

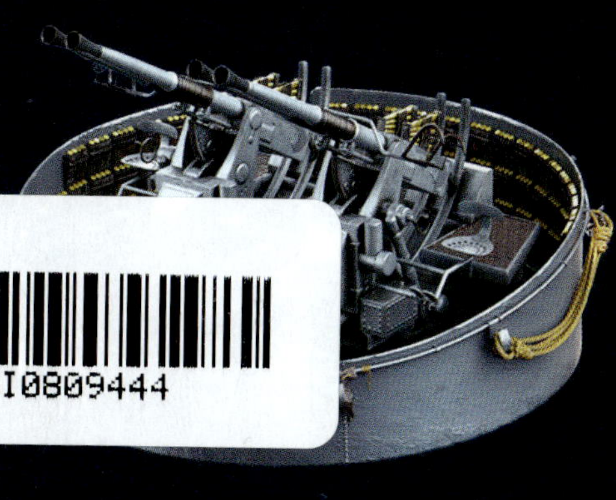

The 40-mm Bofors was produced in a variety of versions: with air and water cooling; in twin, quadruple, and single mounts; with manual aiming; and with power drive. More than ten thousand mounts were manufactured for the Navy and Coast Guard and more than twenty thousand for the Army, and around nine thousand were supplied to allied countries. USS *Massachusetts* was equipped with seven quad-mounted 40-mm Bofors during World War II.

Warships players can battle on more than 40 maps. There are seven different permanent or seasonal Battle Types to choose from: Co-op Battles, Random Battles, Ranked Battles, Clan Battles, Brawls, Scenarios, and Training. Additionally, within Battle Types there are four different Battle Modes available: Standard, Domination, Epicenter, and Arms Race.

Massachusetts made her *World of Warships* PC debut in June 2018 as an American tier VIII; since then she has become a fan favorite. Her decent armor, speed, and guns make her a formidable opponent. In-game, her guns are less accurate than her sister, *Alabama*, but it is her dual-purpose 5-inch battery that really shines. *Massachusetts* has some of the best secondary battery performance in the game—enemy ships really need to think twice before approaching her. *Massachusetts* was removed from sale on PC in early 2021, but she is still available in *World of Warships: Legends*—on console. See *Massachusetts* in person, then take her into battle today in *World of Warships*.

Developed by the team behind *World of Warships* for PC, *World of Warships: Legends* is a completely new entry in Wargaming's flagship nautical franchise that takes full advantage of the power and capabilities of home consoles. *World of Warships: Legends* brings the online naval action loved by millions to home consoles for the very first time, alongside a host of content and features exclusive to the console experience. *World of Warships: Legends* is now available for download from the PlayStation® Store and Microsoft Store. Players can now wage wars across a variety of maps, in numerous warships, and enjoy stunning oceanic vistas with glorious HDR support on PlayStation®4 and Xbox One X. Full 4K support is available on PlayStation®4 Pro, PlayStation®5, and Xbox One X too! *Legends* also supports standard high-def on PlayStation®4 and Xbox One, with more intriguing graphics on the horizon.

Wargaming proudly supports various charitable causes that members of the gaming and history community care deeply about. Supporting veterans and servicemembers: Operation Lifeboat (2020) raised $150,000 USD for Stack Up's mental health awareness helpline; Remembrance charity drive

CONTENTS

Library of Congress Control Number: 2021946729

Bow-on view of the USS *Massachusetts* (BB-59) as she moves beneath the Braga Bridge at Fall River, Massachusetts, with tugs on either side, 12 June 1965.

INTRODUCTION

THIS IS THE BIOGRAPHY OF A BATTLESHIP. The USS *Massachusetts* (BB-59) was the third vessel in the *South Dakota* class. Her massive 16-inch guns were the first of their type to fire in anger during World War II, and they also held the distinction of discharging the last 16-inch salvos of the war. Her shells fell on targets from Casablanca to Tokyo, reflecting her great range and flexibility as a weapon system. She engaged an enemy battleship and protected the most important American amphibious operation of the war, but she spent the majority of her career shepherding the fast carriers of the U.S. Navy from one strike to the next, from one landing operation to the next. In this role, she participated in most major operations of the Pacific War from mid-1943 on. She earned 11 battle stars, and her story is the story of the U.S. Navy's unprecedented triumph in World War II.

This work is based mainly on the *Massachusetts*'s war diary and the reports filed by her captain or executive officer after major actions. It is supplemented by the reports of the ships she protected, and in certain cases by the reports filed by the enemies she fought. Color has been provided by the oral histories recorded by her crew members and preserved by the Battleship Cove Museum in Fall River, Massachusetts, where the historic ship continues her career as an ambassador of education and peace. Portions of articles or sections of works from the U.S. Naval Institute's *Proceedings* and *Naval History* magazines and from books published by the Naval Institute Press have been selectively incorporated as sidebars to further illustrate the *Massachusetts*'s career or to give context to her actions. As this is a popular work, no attempt has been made to source the various quotes used throughout; with very few exceptions they come from the sources mentioned above.

The USS *Massachusetts* on the slip. The workers seen looking down from the stern are seven stories high. (U.S. Navy)

A SHIP IS BORN

WORKERS AT THE BETHLEHEM FORE RIVER SHIPYARD IN QUINCY, Massachusetts, laid the keel of battleship number 59, the third ship in the South Dakota class, on 20 July 1939—barely a month before the German invasion of Poland started what would become World War II. The task of assembling the material for this project was enormous, but working with a sense of urgency caused by the perilous international scene, the shipyard completed the hull, the basic superstructure, and the engine and boiler arrangements in just over two years. Battleship 59, the USS *Massachusetts*, was launched on 23 September 1941, two and a half months before the Japanese attack on Pearl Harbor propelled the United States into the war.

The United States was building its next generation of fast battleships literally just in time.

On 21 May 1942, the U.S. Navy took delivery of the new ship and commissioned the *Massachusetts* at the South Boston Navy Yard Annex, with Francis E. M. Whiting as her first captain and Commander Edward M. Thompson as executive officer. She continued fitting out, uncompleted items were worked through, and the ship reported for duty to the Atlantic Fleet on 10 July. She commenced her first voyage to Casco Bay, Maine, on the 12th.

It is a long process to take a completed ship fresh from the builders and ready her for active service. Such a complicated machine always will have items that require adjustment, repair, or modification, but even more important is the crew. Men must be gathered, trained, and grown accustomed to their new assignment. Competence and teamwork do not happen overnight, especially in a vessel as massive as a battleship. In the case of the *Massachusetts*, the crew had a mix of veterans and reservists, but 70 percent were draftees. Of the ship's 113 officers, only 19 had more than two years' service and 22 had never been to sea. Captain Whiting established a routine whereby his crew stood at general quarters for an hour each day and spent the rest of the day, from before sunrise to 2200, in gunnery drills and exercising damage control, abandon ship, and other tasks. After her run up to Maine, the *Massachusetts* returned to the yard on 21 July for post-trial inspections and more work. Finally, on 2 August, according to her war diary, she sailed from Boston for the Chesapeake Bay for "training, deperming and degaussing calibration, compass and radio direction finder work."

Between 3 August and 28 September the *Massachusetts* made short training cruises and spent ten days in dry dock before reporting for duty in Task Group 21.3 at Hampton Roads, Virginia. She stopped in Annapolis the first weekend in October so the U.S. Naval Academy's midshipmen could visit the fleet's newest battleship. From there she returned to Casco Bay, and then on the 16th, back to Boston to load oil, stores, and ammunition, a process that took three days. She anchored in Casco Bay on 20 October and the next day, Rear Admiral Robert C. Giffen transferred to the *Massachusetts* along with his staff and formed Task Group 34.1. Big events were afoot. In July the United States had determined to invade French North Africa and allocated the brand-new *Massachusetts* to this operation. She would be the big muscle for Task Force 34, an amphibious assault force, poised to strike Morocco in a

The *Massachusetts* being nudged alongside the fitting-out dock by five tugs shortly after launch. (U.S. Navy)

transoceanic thrust across the submarine-infested waters of the central Atlantic. The *Massachusetts* would lead American's first offensive operation in the European-African theater of operations.

On 25 October, a rainy Sunday morning, the *Massachusetts* weighed anchor in patchy fog and proceeded with Cruiser Division 7 (Crudiv), the heavy cruisers *Tuscaloosa* (CA-37) and *Wichita* (CA-45), and Destroyer Division 8 (Desdiv), the *Wainwright* (DD-419), *Mayrant* (DD-402), *Rhind* (DD-404), and *Jenkins* (DD-407). The squadron proceeded south at 15 knots to rendezvous with the loaded transports coming from Hampton Roads. This vitally important operation of war would serve as the battleship's shakedown cruise.

New crewmen practicing ammunition drill. The majority of the ship's crew were teenagers brand new to the Navy and had to learn their jobs from scratch. (U.S. Navy)

Captain Francis Whiting on the quarterdeck. Whiting was promoted to rear admiral shortly after the *Massachusetts*'s successful deployment to Africa. (U.S. Navy)

The *Massachusetts* passing through the Fore River Bridge for her first underway trials. The crew can be seen clustered topside, apparently appreciating the stately progress of their new vessel. (U.S. Navy)

The *South Dakota* Design

From the launching of HMS *Dreadnought* in 1906, battleships were the world's single most powerful and expensive weapon. A navy's strength, even its significance, was measured by the number of battleships it possessed. After the Great War, the major naval powers acted to avoid another crushingly expensive battleship building race, which some perceived as being responsible for the war, by agreeing to restrict the construction of battleships. The new construction that was allowed under the Washington Naval Treaty limited the size of battleships to 35,000 tons standard displacement and their guns to a caliber of 16 inches (406-mm). The art of ship design involves compromise, and in the case of battleships the tradeoffs between characteristics, armament, speed, and protection on the one

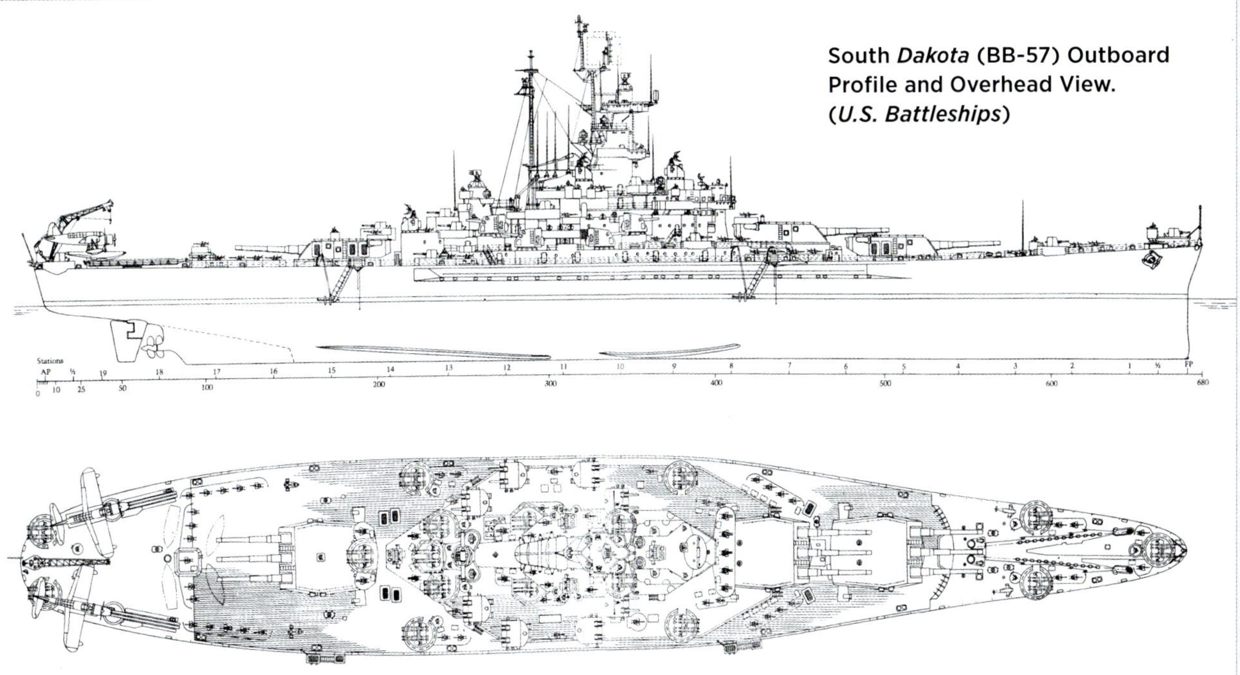

South *Dakota* (BB-57) Outboard Profile and Overhead View. (*U.S. Battleships*)

hand and weight on the other really becomes a juggling act. It was impossible to design a ship with high speed, heavy armor, and the most powerful guns all within a limit of 35,000 tons. Some signatory nations, such as Italy, cheated and constructed the *Littorio* class, a 35,000-ton ship with a good mix of speed, armor, and armament, but an actual displacement of 41,000 tons. The British built the *King George* class, a ship with good armor and speed, but a main armament of only 14-inch guns compared with the U.S. standard of 16-inch and the French, German, and Italian 15-inch armed battleships. This difference is more than it seems, as a 14-inch shell is 1,590 pounds compared to 1,764 for the German 15-inch, and 2,700 pounds for the shell fired by the *Massachusetts's* 16-inch guns. The French *Richelieu* had good speed and decent armor on 35,000 tons, but saved weight by squeezing its main battery forward with eight guns in only two turrets. The *South Dakota*'s design allowed for superior firepower and armor compared to the British, French, German, and Italian "fast battleships" but at the cost of several knots in speed. She had other design compromises; being shorter than the *North Carolina* (BB-55) that preceded her, she was cramped. Habitability was relatively poor, at least by U.S. standards, and she was very wet forward. However, she was handy for a ship of her size and did not suffer from the vibration problems that plagued the *North Carolina*.

(ADAPTED FROM DULIN AND GARZKE, *BATTLESHIPS*, 1985 - NAVAL INSTITUTE PRESS, AND FRIEDMAN, *US BATTLESHIPS*, 1985 - NAVAL INSTITUTE PRESS)

***Massachusetts* Inboard Profile. (Dulin and Garzke)**

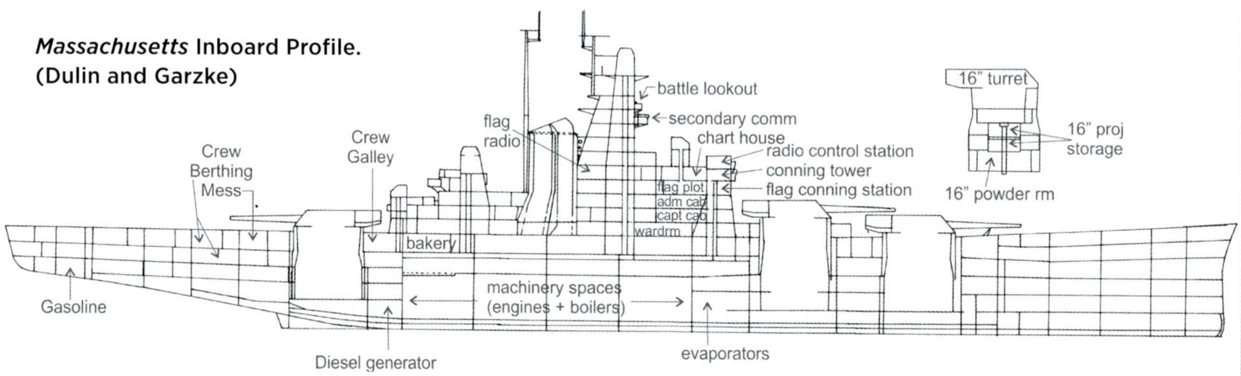

Armament

The *South Dakota* class mounted the new 16-inch/45-caliber Mark 6 gun in three triple turrets, each of which weighed 1,437 tons. Guns were mounted in separate sleeves allowing individual elevation and depression.

The basic characteristics were:

Training gear rate:	4°/second
Elevation rate:	12°/second
Maximum elevation:	45°
Firing cycle:	30 seconds
Designed capacity:	1,280 rounds
Shell weight (lbs/kg):	2,700/1,225
Muzzle Velocity (fps/ms):	2,300/701
Maximum range (yds/m):	36,900/33,741

1. Range finder
2. Breech block (open)
3. Chain rammer
4. Pan floor
5. Center projectile hoist
6. Left projectile hoist
7. Roller path
8. Powder hoist
9. Powder car
10. Electric deck
11. Elevating cylinder

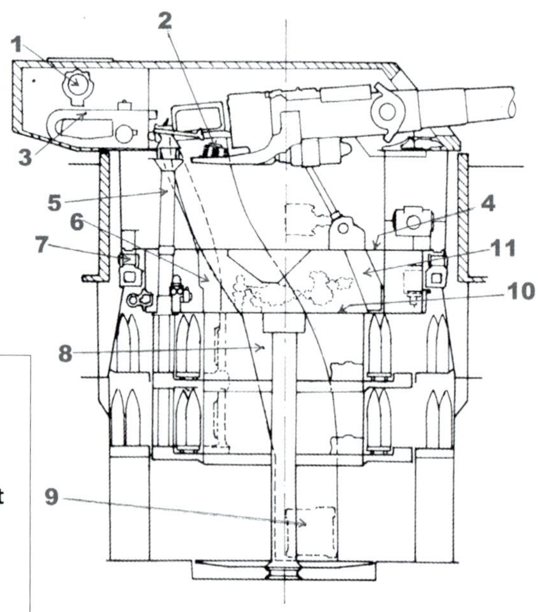

MK 6 16-inch turret. (*Naval Weapons*)

(ADAPTED FROM DULIN AND GARZKE, *BATTLESHIPS*, 1985 - NAVAL INSTITUTE PRESS, AND CAMPBELL, *NAVAL WEAPONS OF WWII*, 1985 - NAVAL INSTITUTE PRESS)

The secondary armament consisted of ten twin mounted 5-inch/38 Mark 12 dual-purpose guns. The Pacific Fleet Ordnance Board described the Mark 12 as "outstandingly accurate, fast-firing and easy to maintain, with a long barrel life."

5-inch gun. (*Naval Weapons*)

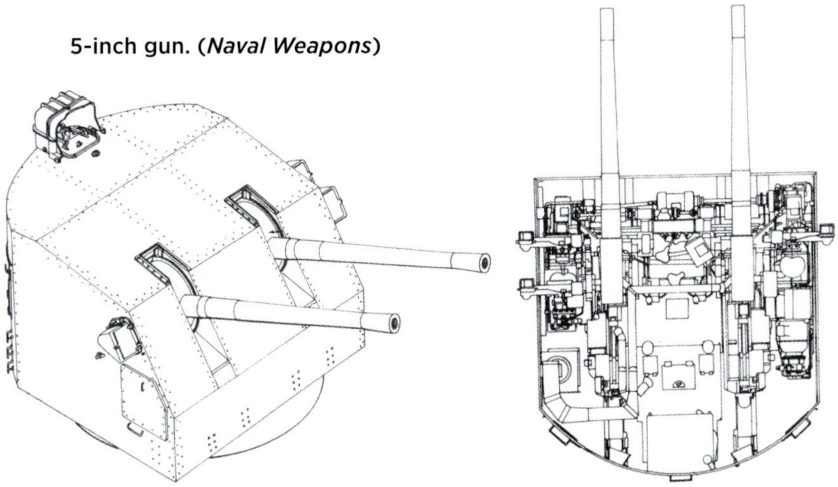

Its basic characteristics were:

Training speed:	25°/second
Elevation rate:	15°/second
Maximum elevation:	85°
Firing cycle:	3 seconds
Ammunition carried:	9,600 rounds or 480 rounds/gun
Shell weight (lbs/kg):	53.85/24.43
Muzzle Velocity (fps/ms):	2,600/792
Maximum range (yds/m):	17,575/16,070

The antiaircraft battery was designed without the benefit of wartime experience, and by 1940 the Navy recognized the inadequacy of the short-range batteries in the original design. These consisted of three quad 1.1-inch mountings and a dozen 0.50-caliber machine guns. Fortunately, there was time to improve these arrangements. As constructed, the *Massachusetts* had six quadruple 40-mm mounts and 35 single 20-mm guns. She added four more quadruple 40-mm mounts after her return from Africa and two more in February 1943 for a total of a dozen mounts and 48 barrels. By this date the *Massachusetts* had added another 26 20-mm guns for a total of 61 barrels. She went to the Pacific with this outfit. War experience led to further modifications, and by late 1944 she possessed 18 quadruple 40-mm mounts (72 barrels) and 38 20-mm barrels.

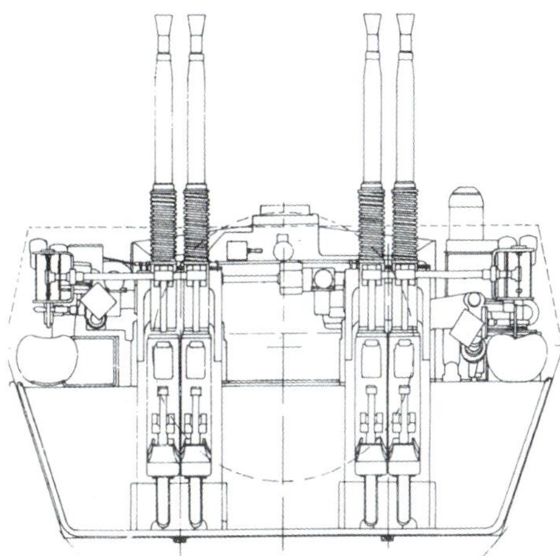

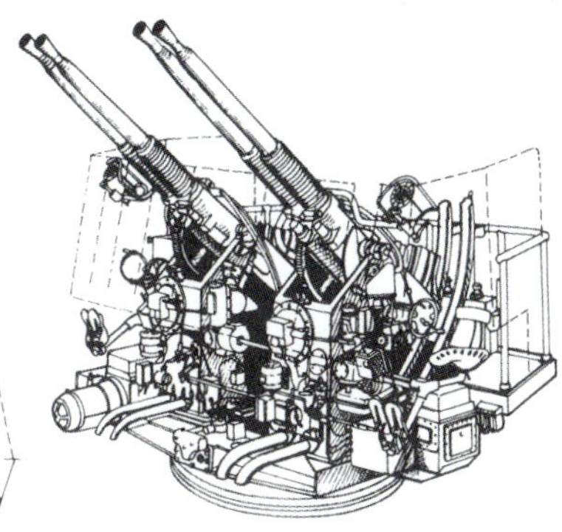

40-mm gun. (*Naval Weapons*)

Characteristics 40-mm:

Shell weight (lbs/kg):	1.985/0.9
Muzzle Velocity (fps/ms):	2,890/881
Ceiling at (ft/m):	22,800/10,060
Maximum range (yds/m):	11,000/10,058

The 20-mm Oerlikon was a popular Swedish design used by the Americans, the British, the Italians, and the Germans, among others.

As the war wore on, many considered the Oerlikon too light to meet the needs of fleet air defense—especially in the face of the Kamikaze threat. There was a saying that "When the 20-mm opens fire it's time to hit the deck." Nonetheless, the gun remained in use throughout the war.

In U.S. service its characteristics were:

Shell weight (lbs/kg):	.2714/0.1231
Muzzle Velocity (fps/ms):	2,740/835
Rate of Fire:	450 rounds/minute
Ceiling at (ft/m):	10,000/3,050
Maximum range (yds/m):	4,800/4,390

Armor

The reason the U.S. Navy Bureau of Ships (BuShips) designed the *South Dakotas* in the first place and did not build more *North Carolinas* was to improve the armor protection. They accomplished this with no sacrifice in speed or firepower, and the design, in this respect, must be considered successful although the gains came, as always, at a cost. The design's biggest innovation was the placement of the boilers above the engines. This reduced the ship's overall length, at no sacrifice in speed, and reduced the area that required protection—another weight savings.

The protection scheme was designed to withstand 16-inch shellfire. Against the older 2,240-pound shell the immunity zone was calculated as from 17,700 to 30,900 yards. Against the newer 2,700-pound shell this became 20,500 to 26,400 yards.

The armor characteristics were:

Side armor: 12.2 inches with 19 degree inclination from the vertical. The lower belt extended down through the underwater protective system, tapering from 12.2 inches at the top to 1 inch at the bottom to protect against large shells hitting below the waterline.

Main deck:	1.5 inches
Second deck:	5.75 inches
Splinter deck:	0.625 inches
Third deck:	0.3 inches
Steering gear third deck armor:	6.2 inches
Turrets:	18-inch face plates, 9.5-inch sides, 12-inch backs, and 7.25-inch tops
Barbette:	17.3 to 11.6 inches
Conning tower sides and communications tube:	16 inches
Conning tower roof:	7.25 inches

ADAPTED FROM DULIN AND GARZKE, *BATTLESHIPS*, 1985 - NAVAL INSTITUTE PRESS.

Machinery

Design studies established that a 30-knot maximum speed would require more than 200,000-shaft horsepower and a hull appreciably longer than that of the *North Carolina* class. This was not possible at a displacement of 35,000 tons given the requirements of nine 16-inch guns and enhanced armor. Thus, the Navy accepted 27.5 knots as a design goal.

The class was equipped with four sets of geared turbines and eight Somers-type boilers. These employed stream pressure of 600 psi at a temperature of 850° F. The propulsion plant arrangement had four main machinery spaces with two air-encased boilers, one set of geared turbines, and auxiliary equipment in each compartment. This allowed the main propulsion

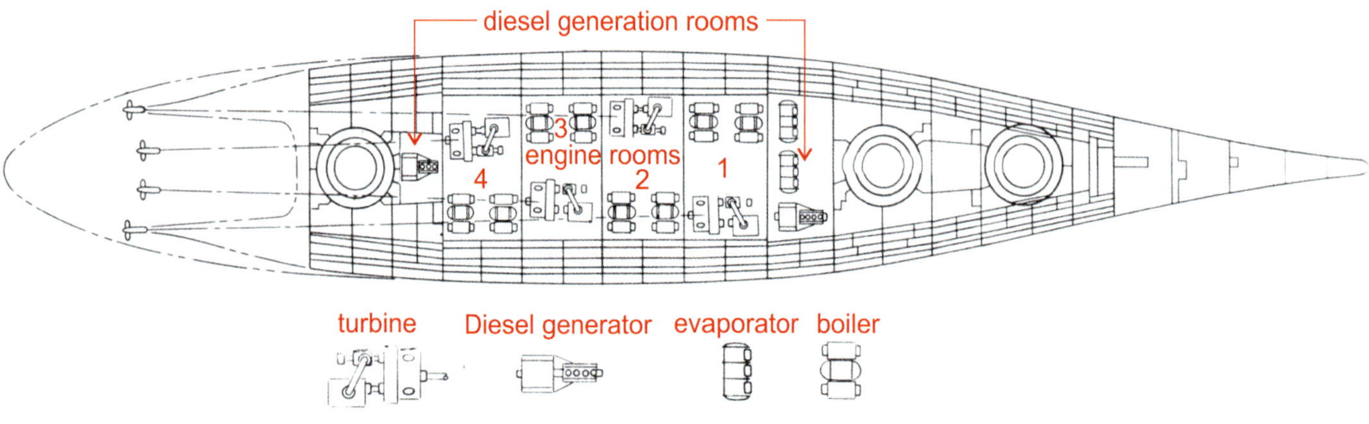

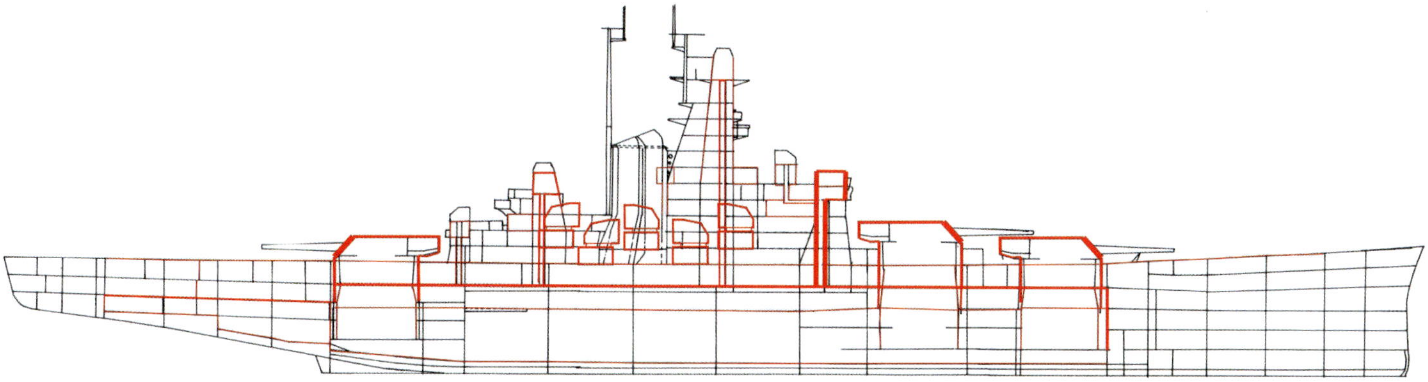

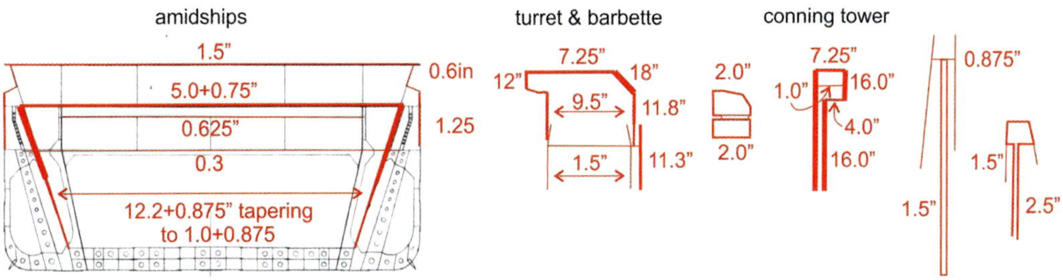

The designers considered the *Massachusetts*'s side protection better than that of the *North Carolina* class. It consisted of four bulkheads parallel to the side shell. The two outboard compartments normally were liquid loaded at all times, while the two inboard compartments were void. The internal sloping armor of the side belt was expected to reduce the deflection of the holding bulkhead. This allowed the number of bulkheads to be reduced by one with a corresponding reduction in the system's breadth. With tanks outboard of the armor belt, the gas jet from an underwater detonation could be somewhat vented upward, thus moderating the forces on the inboard bulkheads. The side protection of this class was never tested in action.

machinery to be completely isolated and consequently improved overall resistance to damage. The boilers in machinery rooms 1 and 3 were to port with the turbines to starboard. Rooms 2 and 4 had the opposite arrangement. The boilers were elevated sufficiently above the inner bottom to provide for better shaft clearances than in the *North Carolina* class. The evaporators were located forward of machinery room 1.

The high-pressure, high-temperature steam cycle made it possible to increase normal maximum shaft horsepower. The close proximity of the forward tower and the uptakes permitted mutual structural support and protection, a feature repeated in subsequent designs.

Shaft horsepower:	**135,000 (136,872 mhp)**
Weight:	**3,580 (3,637 metric tons)**
Pounds per horsepower:	**59.4 (26.57 kg/mhp)**

Radar

The *South Dakota* class was designed before the development of practical shipborne radar and the Navy first specified installation of radar in the summer of 1941. Initially the *Massachusetts* was equipped with an SC air search on the mainmast, and an SG surface search radar on a platform ahead of the forward main battery director and a second SG on the mainmast. The main and secondary batteries also used radar for fire control with a pair of F.D. Mark 3 radars for the Mk 38 Main Battery Director and four F.C. Mark 4s for the Mark 37 Secondary Battery Directors. The *Massachusetts* went to war in Africa with this outfit, but the Mark 3s were replaced by the F.C. Mark 8 before her Pacific deployment. Whereas the Mark 3 could return an accurate range, it had a broad spread and could not give useful bearings. This required optical input to determine and correct. The Mark 8's improvement was a "B" scope presentation of targets in a plot of range versus bearing. Thus, this system promised accurate surface fire under complete radar control during night engagements. In her only surface action against enemy warships the *Massachusetts* experienced failures or inaccuracies in all fire control radars. Her success in hitting the French warships *Jean Bart* at 25,000 yards and *Milan*, which was under way, at 28,000 yards was attained using optical systems in conditions of intermittent to poor visibility. Radar problems continued to plague the *Massachusetts* even during shore bombardment missions later in the war.

Captain Whiting's comments after the bombardment of Casablanca and the subsequent naval battle are telling: "It is recommended that these fire control sets be shock tested and vibration tested, to determine the cause of the numerous failures in the 10 ampere fuses. Nearly every set had these fuses blow during the firing. Under normal conditions they seem satisfactory, but under gun fire (own ship's) they seem to fail very easily. These fire control sets are still too complicated and touchy for the concussion and shock they are subjected to. Whenever something goes out, too much time is lost in finding the failure. One thing such as loss of the ranges notch can be caused by at least three different tube failures, with the consequent testing of three different circuits, to find the failures."

(ADAPTED FROM FRIEDMAN, *US BATTLESHIPS*, 1985 - NAVAL INSTITUTE PRESS)

Counting Beans

Construction of a ship such as the *Massachusetts* was not only a marvel of engineering and organization, it required mighty feats of accounting by both the Bureau of Ships and Bethlehem Steel, the company constructing the vessel. Payment was made in monthly installments, with Bethlehem submitting a voucher that BuShips carefully scrutinized and then passed along to the Judge Advocate General of the Navy for payment. The November 1940 voucher, for example, was for $498,150. This voucher included material and labor for 40 line items such as drawings, piping, pumps, and compressed air system, giving the total estimated cost and the amount expended to date. The total cost of drawings, for example, was $450,000 for materials and $450,000 for labor, of which, by November 1940, $97,500 had been charged. Pumps were $381,500 for material but only $19,900 for labor. The entire amount was still outstanding in November. The ship's machinery cost was nearly $15 million, and the estimated total cost $77 million.

The Navy, it should be noted, was a good customer. Bethlehem Steel submitted the November 1940 voucher on 10 December 1940. BuShips completed its review and approved payment in less than a week. Considering that in November 1940 the Navy had 8 battleships, 1 aircraft carrier, 4 cruisers, and more than 20 destroyers under construction, this speaks of a bureaucracy that could get things done.

Accounting included more than just finances: More important for the ship's ultimate purpose of engaging in successful operations was keeping track of all the many construction defects or improvements that the ship required. Many of these items only could be discovered once the ship was complete and the crew was engaged in readying the vessel for active operations. For example, on 20 July Captain Whiting wrote to BuShips requesting permission to cut 6 inches off the armored splinter deck next to Hatch 2-102 because when going through this hatch "the head must be ducked in order to pass the splinter deck without hitting it. To date several men have received head injuries in hurrying down the hatch to their battle stations." This request generated a work order to the Commandant of the Boston Navy Yard on 8 August with copies to the other ships in the class, which presumably were experiencing a similar problem. In early June 1942 hot weather in New England revealed a more serious problem. ". . . the inadequacy of sheathing and ventilation in living spaces has come to attention. The temperature has been sufficient to trip the magazine fire alarms which functions at 105° F." In this case Captain Whiting only could throw the problem at BuShips and request that immediate remedial steps be taken.

Through 16 July, when the *Massachusetts* was recommended for acceptance, the contractor had accomplished 90 of 115 such improvements, "undertaking work not a part of the contract but which could be accomplished at the building rather than the outfitting yard." Of course, every change order and every job undertaken, no matter how trivial, generated an invoice.

Expanding the Fleet

One of the Navy's great accomplishments during the war was the way it rose to the challenge of manning its vastly expanded fleet with competent officers and quality crews.

The Navy traditionally filled its ranks with volunteers. During the Great Depression of the 1930s, there was a surplus of young men seeking to join, and the Navy could accept only those candidates who had a high school diploma or equivalent. This led to a highly trained cadre of recruits, giving the service some of the most capable enlisted men in its history. The available surplus facilitated the Navy's rapid increase in size during the last years of peace. In 1939 the authorized strength was increased to 145,000 men; by the time of Pearl Harbor the number in service had grown to 337,000. On V-J Day, 2 September 1945, the Navy had 2.995 million men. When the *Massachusetts* was laid down, there were 178 surface warships in the navy and 380 total active vessels. On 14 August the count was 833 surface warships and 6,768 total active vessels.

The situation with officers was far different. The primary source of new officers was the U.S. Naval Academy, and although graduating classes were larger than the number of officers retiring, there were not enough officers to meet peacetime demands, let alone those of war. This problem was particularly acute at higher grades. The number of officers that could be promoted to higher ranks was based on a percentage of officers available, not the number of open positions.

In 1935 the authorized strength of the officer corps was 6,531, but only 6,320 were in service. Nearly 8,000 would be needed to meet the requirements of new construction. The number of authorized officers was increased again in 1938, but as the size of the fleet continued to grow, the officer count lagged behind. The dramatic increase in the size of the Navy authorized in 1940 invalidated all prior approaches to resolving the issue and forced the temporary augmentation of the regular officer corps with reserve, retired, and fitted officers. This measure, however, was still insufficient to meet the needs of wartime expansion. Reserve officers were provided through the Naval Reserve Officers Training Corps (NROTC). Established in 1925, the program grew from humble beginnings to a large program during the war. There were nine civilian universities participating in 1940, which produced about 200 reserve ensigns a year. By 1945, 52 universities participated and the number of graduating officers had increased tenfold. There were 35,760 officers on active duty on 7 December 1941 and, at the peak in June 1945, 198,383 officers.

(ADAPTED FROM *O'HARA ET AL, ON SEAS CONTESTED*, 215, 2010 - NAVAL INSTITUTE PRESS)

New recruits drill at the San Diego Naval Training Center. At the start of the war the Navy operated training centers in San Diego, California; Great Lakes, Illinois; Bainbridge, Maryland; and Newport, Rhode Island. During the war the Navy opened three more centers at Norfolk, Virginia; Sampson, New York; and Farragut, Idaho. These centers met the Navy's tremendous personnel needs by transforming civilians into sailors in roughly six weeks. (U.S. Naval Institute Photo Archive)

The USS *Massachusetts* in an official wartime photograph. (U.S. Navy)

USS *Massachusetts* as Completed

- Launched 23 September 1941
- Commissioned 20 March 1942/ Operational August 1942
- 680′10″ overall length
- 666′ 0″ waterline length
- 108′ 2.25″ maximum beam
- 28′7” mean draft @ 35,000 tons
- 36′9” maximum draft @ 47,000 tons
- 35,113 tons light
- 43,884 tons optimum battle load
- 45,216 tons full load
- Nine 16-inch/45-caliber Mark 6 in three turrets
- 20 5-inch/38-caliber Mark 12 in ten mounts
- 24 40-mm/56-caliber in six mounts (by December 1944 72 guns in 18 mounts)
- 35 20-mm/70-caliber in 35 mounts (by December 1944 38 guns)
- Fuel oil 6,876 tons; diesel 157.1 tons; gasoline 23.8 tons
- Speed 27.5 knots at 130,000 mph
- Endurance: 17,000 nm @ 15 knots; 6,400 nm @ 25 knots

A rogue wave upended one of the *Massachusetts*'s Kingfisher floatplanes, forcing her to enter her first combat with just two aircraft. (U.S. Navy)

TORCH

IN JULY 1942 THE UNITED STATES AGREED TO INVADE FRENCH NORTH AFRICA in conjunction with British forces. Dubbed Operation Torch by British Prime Minister Winston Churchill, this venture, launched from bases in the United States and Great Britain, included an audacious transoceanic landing on the shores of Morocco. The invasion force, commanded by Rear Admiral H. Kent Hewitt, was named Task Force 34. The elements of TF 34 included amphibious task groups 34.8 and 34.10, which departed Hampton Roads, Virginia, on 23 October and headed southeast. The next day another amphibious force, TG 34.9, left Hampton Roads as if bound for Great Britain. The *Massachusetts*, flagship of Rear Admiral Robert C. Giffen, led Task Group 34.1, including two heavy cruisers and four destroyers, from Casco Bay, Maine, the same day. These task groups—along with a carrier group, TG 34.2, with the *Ranger* (CV-4), three escort carriers, a light cruiser, and nine destroyers—rendezvoused in the east central Atlantic on the 28th. The three amphibious groups embarked the U.S. 3rd Division for landings at Fédala, near Casablanca; the 9th Division's 60th Regimental Combat Team (RCT) for landings at Port Lyautey north of Rabat; and the 47th RCT with Combat Command B of the 2nd Armored Division for landings at Safi, southwest of Casablanca. Major General George C. Patton commanded the ground forces.

The planners had worried about submarines, but the American force never came within a thousand miles of a U-boat attack. The biggest concern turned out to be weather. Rough seas made refueling impossible, and by mid-ocean the bunkers on some of the small vessels were nearing empty. Even the *Massachusetts*, normally the most stable platform in any sea, suffered a mishap when a rogue wave broke over the fantail and upended one of the ship's Kingfishers.

Fortunately, the weather moderated as the Americans neared Africa. The smaller ships were able to fuel, and at 0700 on 7 November Hewett made the flag signal "proceed on service assigned," and the Central Group turned toward Casablanca. Fifteen transports would land troops of the 3rd Division at Fédala under the *Massachusetts*'s protection.

The battleship's crew went to breakfast at 0400 hours on the morning of 8 November and then proceeded to battle stations. A general mood of anxiety pervaded the ship. From Rear Admiral Giffen down to the youngest of the new recruits (who was just 15, having used forged papers to join the Navy), no one knew if the French would resist.

The Americans based their hopes of a peaceful operation on a French dissident group, which included military and civilian elements, that wanted to rejoin the war on the American side. As it happened, this group had little support in Morocco, and all its attempted putsch accomplished was to alert the French command that something was up. When French naval headquarters in Casablanca began receiving reports of strange events offshore, such as the sound of motorboats, it leapt to the assumption that the allies were conducting a commando attack in conjunction with the suppressed coup d'état. It had no idea that an American armada was just offshore waiting for dawn, nor that thousands of troops were even at that moment motoring to landing beaches at three widely separated locations in Morocco.

As the *Massachusetts*'s crew assembled to general quarters and the ship's two Kingfishers waited on the catapults ready to be launched (and to scout for the white flags the pilots had been told to look for), the port of Casablanca was crowded with civilian and military shipping. On the evening of 7 November a major convoy had just arrived from the French West African base at Dakar, and three more were expected. Civilians, largely women and children, evacuated from Dakar, were disembarking from the large liner *Protros*, which was docked at the end of the Quai Delinde, just yards from the French battleship *Jean Bart*. This powerful ship had been towed to Casablanca following the collapse of France in June 1940. She could not get under way, but had modern fire control and a turret of four 15-inch guns in service, making her a very powerful shore battery. Other French naval forces in Casablanca consisted of a light cruiser, 3 large destroyers (1 under repair), 7 fleet destroyers, 1 large and 2 small sloops, and 11 submarines.

At 0530, as civilian ships unloaded, French Vice Admiral François Michelier ordered five submarines to sea to determine what was happening offshore. An hour later, one of the subs reported the blinding flashes of large naval guns off Fédala, a fishing port 12 miles up the coast. At 0630, as more reports began flooding French headquarters, Michelier ordered his surface forces to raise steam and attack the intruders, whoever they might be. Dawn was still 20 minutes away, and a thick haze smothered the shoreline.

As French warships prepared for sea, Task Group 34.1 was 15 miles off Casablanca with the *Massachusetts* in the van followed by the *Tuscaloosa* and *Wichita*. The destroyers *Wainwright* and *Mayrant* screened to starboard and the *Rhind* and *Jenkins* to port. The carrier fighters and bombers commenced roaring off flight decks at 0615, but even before that TG 34.1 started launching its own aircraft. The *Tuscaloosa* and *Wichita* catapulted seven Curtiss SOC Seagulls for spotting and antisubmarine patrol. The *Massachusetts* launched her two Kingfishers at 0618 and 0620.

The planes arrived over the city, and several radioed that enemy submarines and destroyers were standing out to sea. They had hardly delivered this surprising news when French fighters appeared. Robert Etheridge, flying as a Kingfisher radioman, recalled, "We circled the *Jean Bart* at 5,000 feet when the war started. We had only been over our target for five or ten minutes when enemy fighters approached, so we started evasive action. Tom [Thomas Doherty, the ship's senior aviator] was a super pilot. He could slip to the side and get down to a lower level and sometimes the fighters couldn't get down that low. Anyway, the fighters missed twice. I think it was the third time when he hit us with a lot of shells, and at that time Tom knew we had to take

The USS *Ranger* followed by a pair of *Gleaves*-class destroyers at dusk of the first day's operations off Morocco. (Library of Congress)

Casablanca Harbor, crowded with shipping. This photo shows the French destroyer *Tempête* with a patrol vessel alongside moored along the harbor's outer jetty. The El Hank light and battery are visible in the background. (U.S. Navy)

evasive action and find a place to land before we were gonna crash. So he spotted this beach not too far, just up north of town. It looked like a good clean beach, but as we were approaching there the engine quit and we crashed. . . . we were probably 100 yards off the beach." Etheridge was wounded in the hard landing. French soldiers helped the two aviators ashore and took them prisoner.

The battleship's other Kingfisher also had a close call. At 0659 it radioed the battleship: "Am coming in on starboard bow with couple hostile aircraft on my tail. Pick them off—I am the one in front." The *Massachusetts* obliged with 35 5-inch rounds, and other ships joined in.

At 0705 the major shore battery just south of Casablanca, El Hank, loosed a four 7.64-inch gun salvo at the *Massachusetts* from 27,000 yards. These events made it clear that the French were going to resist. This caught most crewmen by surprise. "We were standing there behind the 16-inch guns, all a sudden I looked up I saw sprays. Purple colors, red colors, orange colors, so I said to the bosun's mate, 'What's the cause of that?' And he said, 'Hit the deck, the French are shooting at us.'" The French used dye to color the geysers thrown up by their shells. The technique assisted spotting, especially in cases where more than one ship was firing at the same target.

As colored gouts of water splashed nearby, the *Massachusetts* turned 40 degrees away and a minute later opened fire on the *Jean Bart* from 24,400 yards. With this salvo, the *Massachusetts* fired the very first 16-inch shells by an American warship at an enemy target. At 0708 the *Jean Bart* answered. Her first two-round salvo raised giant yellow splashes 600 yards off the *Massachusetts*'s starboard bow. The next, fired at 0711, fell close to port. El Hank's aim was also good. The battleship's chronology recorded "very large" yellow and green splashes falling "close aboard" to starboard at 0711 and to port at 0713. However, the French could barely discern their targets, and the *Jean Bart* only fired two more salvos for the rest of the day, one of two rounds at 0716 and the last of one round at 0719.

The Americans had targeting problems of their own. Smoke enveloped the harbor, and after the third salvo a vacuum tube failure caused the *Massachusetts*'s Fire Control Mk 3 radar to blink out. It was not fixed until that afternoon. Next the massive concussion from the second nine-gun 16-inch salvo blew the fuses on two Mk 4 FD (antiaircraft fire control) radars. Air spot was initially unavailable due to the action of French fighters. For the first 15 minutes the battleship used indirect fire and her gunnery was ineffective. When her surviving Kingfisher did begin to spot, smoke over the harbor affected its observations; it reported range accurately but not deflection. The battleship did not hit until 0725 when a 2,700-pound shell bashed the *Jean Bart* aft on the shelter deck, slicing through two armored decks before exploding in an empty magazine.

The French destroyer squadron was berthed in the line of fire, but remarkably, as they raised steam and recalled men and officers, the operational vessels escaped damage. They masked their movement with smoke as they started to file out of the harbor, but aircraft repeatedly warned the *Massachusetts* that destroyers were getting under way. The flotilla included the large destroyers *Milan* and *Albatros* and the fleet destroyers *Brestois*, *Boulonnais*, *Fougueux*, *Frondeur*, and *L'Alcyon*. The *Tempête* and *Simoun* were repairing hull damage suffered in a collision and could not immediately sail. The large destroyer *Malin*, which had come up from Dakar for a refit, likewise could not get under way. At 0806 a 16-inch shell landed between the *Malin* and the jetty. Enormous splinters riddled the vessel, killing seven. The projectile's cap tore a destructive path 80 feet long, flooding the boiler and engine rooms. The light cruiser *Primauguet* sailed later.

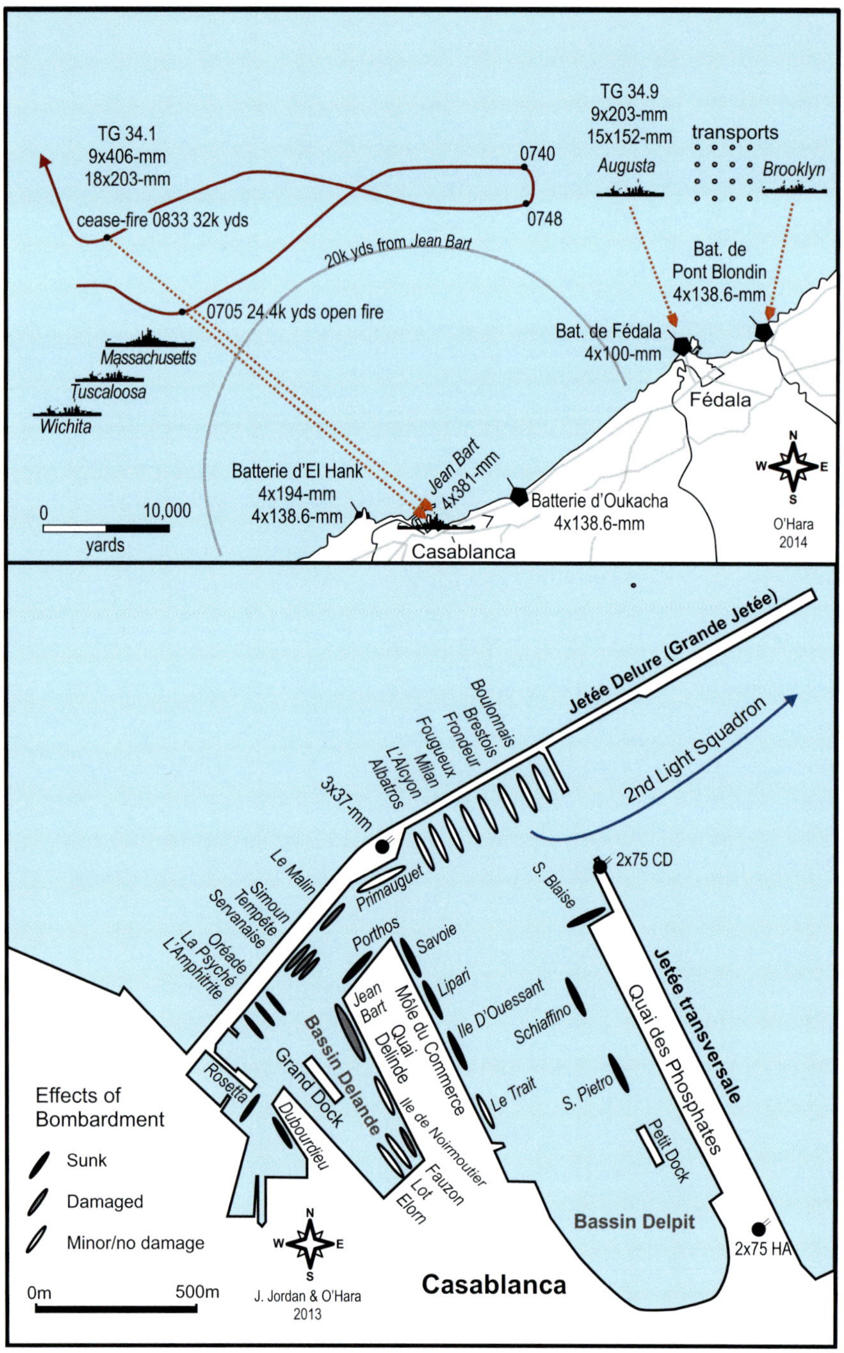

As the French destroyers hastened to sea, the *Massachusetts* started to hit the *Jean Bart* consistently. At 0735 a 16-inch projectile clipped the French battleship's bow, and a minute later another struck the quay, showering the French ship's deck with stone fragments. A minute after that a round punched through the *Jean Bart*'s funnel and angled down into the hull before exiting at the main armored deck; another plowed through the quay wall and hit the main armor belt. The belt deflected the shell down and it exited without exploding.

The bombardment destroyed or damaged much of the commercial

Kingfisher on the catapult. These aircraft served as jacks-of-all-trade, performing reconnaissance, gunnery spotting, rescue work, antisubmarine patrol; providing practice targets for the ships' antiaircraft crews; and even carrying out bombing missions. (U.S. Naval Institute Photo Archive)

shipping in the harbor as well. The newly arrived passenger ships *Porthos*, *Savoie*, and *Lipari* were still crowded with civilian evacuees. They had started disembarking at 0545, and when the first shells came screaming into the harbor the final 400 passengers fled at a run. At 0736 a 16-inch shell smacked the *Porthos*, which was tied to the head of the mole. She capsized, suffering 24 dead. A pair of 16-inch rounds smashed the tanker *Île d'Ouessant* at 0755 and she sank rapidly. The *Fauzon* and *Île de Noirmoutier* were moored behind the *Jean Bart*. Sixteen-inch shells passed through the *Fauzon* at 0800 and 0815, but the ship remained afloat. Another ripped *Île de Noirmoutier* at 0810 and caused major flooding.

At 0806 a 16-inch round ricocheted off *Jean Bart*'s operational turret, carrying away a 90-mm gun mounted alongside; the shell did not explode, but it pushed the glacis plate down and jammed the turret in place. Another shell from the same salvo struck turret No. 2's barbette and broke up. It ricocheted off the main armored deck and penetrated several compartments before coming to rest. Four minutes later a projectile pierced the *Jean Bart*'s quarterdeck forward of the starboard catapult. After ripping through a 100-mm armored deck, the shell exploded in a ballast tank beneath the steering gear. Fragments punched through the ship's bottom.

The El Hank and the smaller Table d'Oukacha battery to the east of the harbor remained fully operational despite being targeted by 69 8-inch and 19 16-inch salvos. The ships were using armor-piercing rather than high-explosive type ammunition, which reduced their effectiveness against such targets. A subsequent analysis called the results disappointing and complained that many of the *Massachusetts*'s rounds were duds (although the Naval Inspector General later disputed this). El Hank targeted mostly the *Massachusetts*. From the battleship's decks it seemed to one participant that "Throughout this action, heavy stuff was whizzing over . . . and splashing in the water close aboard."

At 0830 Rear Admiral Giffen overheard a TBS message that there was no resistance ashore and that the bombardment was killing townspeople. He ordered cease-fire at 0833. This came at a good time for the *Massachusetts*, inasmuch as with salvo 45, fired at 0812, a shell being loaded into Turret 1 tipped and fell through the hoist, jamming the turret, which was training to port at the time. It took 35 minutes to clear. Minor problems with shell supply or mechanics caused one or more guns to misfire during 16 of the 50 salvos discharged during the bombardment.

The Naval Battle of Casablanca

The naval battle of Casablanca was the largest surface, air, and subsurface naval action fought in the Atlantic Ocean during World War II. From first shot to last the battle lasted more than six hours and during that time the U.S. Navy deployed the *Massachusetts*, three heavy cruisers, one light cruiser, and ten destroyers supplemented by carrier fighters, bombers, and a minesweeper (which got accidentally involved); the French had one immobile battleship, three shore batteries, a light cruiser, two large destroyers, seven fleet destroyers, two sloops, a patrol boat, and three submarines. During the battle the French flotilla repeatedly threatened the transports and even broke up a landing with gunfire. Both sides suffered damage during this prolonged action, but the French suffered the most by far. French gunfire from warships and shore batteries moderately damaged the destroyer *Ludlow* and heavy cruiser *Wichita* and did minor damage to the minesweeper *Palmer*, the cruiser *Brooklyn*, and the *Massachusetts*. The French had two destroyers sunk and one light cruiser, two large destroyers, and two destroyers heavily damaged. The other ships engaged all suffered at least minor damage.

Antiaircraft fire chases four French fighters away from an American spotting plane during the early morning hours of the Battle of Casablanca. (U.S. Navy)

Casablanca Harbor, showing the *Jean Bart* and the Lafonde Basin to port of the battleship and the capsized hulk of the *Prothos*, victim of the *Massachusetts*'s heavy guns, bottom left. (U.S. Navy)

The French liner *Prothus*, hit by a 16-inch shell intended for the *Jean Bart*, is capsized at dock. She had arrived in Casablanca early that morning carrying refugees from Dakar. (U.S. Navy)

Shell falling just short of the *Massachusetts* during the battle. The size of the geyser suggests it was fired by El Hank. French guns hit the battleship twice during the action but inflicted only minor damage. (U.S. Naval Institute Photo Archive)

At 0815 the French squadron, two large and five fleet destroyers, started up the coast at 18 knots. Aircraft reported their presence, but the information did not reach Rear Admiral Giffen even though he was responsible for their containment. He was 15 miles away sailing in the opposite direction, trading slow salvos with El Hank. The *Massachusetts*'s chronology notes that at 0817 two submarines were observed leaving Casablanca but says nothing about destroyers. Giffen's report does not address this failure to contain the French squadron. Perhaps the intensity of the bombardment and the smoke roiling up from the harbor made him believe the surface threat had been eliminated. What is certain is that the battleship's absence gave the French a golden opportunity. Their plan was to head up the coast with the rising sun behind them and strike enemy transports reported off Fédala. It was just a 30-minute sail.

At first, the only response to the French intrusion was a group of F4Fs orbiting Fédala waiting a call to action. They spotted the French warships and dropped one-by-one to strafe the enemy column while radioing frantic alerts. In the meantime, the *Milan* spotted unknown destroyers off her port bow. The French formed up and attacked. The ships the *Milan* spotted were the *Wilkes* (DD-441), *Swanson* (DD-443), and *Ludlow* (DD-438). At 0825 the French opened fire from 16,000 yards. The *Wilkes* and *Swanson* retreated north at flank speed. The *Ludlow* zigzagged after them as pink, green, blue, and uncolored geysers spouted around her and a few splinters rattled aboard. Then one of the *Milan*'s 138-mm rounds hit the *Ludlow* and knocked her from the fight.

At 0825 Admiral Hewitt's flagship, the *Augusta* (CA-31), which had been bombarding shore batteries near the landing beaches, turned to engage the French ships. The admiral also jumped on the radio and informed Giffen that enemy warships were off Casablanca. At 0830 the *Milan* trained her battery on landing craft loaded with troops of the 7th Regiment's Company L off Fédala Yellow Beach. She sank one boat and damaged others. This was the only occasion during World War II when loaded American landing craft came under direct fire from a major enemy warship. At this point the *Milan* was just five miles from the *Leonard Wood* (APA-12), the flag transport. Fortunately for the Americans, thick black smoke from a burning oil tank screened her and the other transports from French view. The fact that the strafing aircraft had wounded the French admiral and most of the lookouts may have contributed to the failure to seize such an opportunity. Then, when the *Augusta* and *Brooklyn* (CL-40, the other cruiser supporting the landings) came up, the French reversed course, hoping to lure the Americans toward the big guns of the *Jean Bart* and El Hank.

At 0845, with still no word from Giffen, Hewitt radioed his subordinate: "French Cruisers standing up coast from Casablanca to Fedala. Cover Transports." In fact, Giffen had just ordered cease fire thinking that he had overcome resistance in the city. At 0834 the *Massachusetts* turned north by northwest, still sailing in the wrong direction. At 0848 Giffen radioed Hewitt asking if he desired assistance after observing "what appeared to be two destroyers standing out of Casablanca harbor." Because he was beyond sight of the harbor at this time, he was likely responding to radio chatter about the French sortie. In any case, this was the first indication in any report produced by Giffen or the *Massachusetts* that French warships were in action. Shortly thereafter, Hewitt's 0845 order arrived. It answered Giffen's question, and at 0855 the *Massachusetts* swung her bow toward the east and headed at top speed for Fédala, 35 miles away.

At 0916, after sailing east-southeast for 21 minutes (covering 19,000 yards) the *Massachusetts* spotted enemy ships making heavy smoke off the starboard bow. Her report noted that "it was difficult to ascertain the exact number . . . or to identify them accurately." Nonetheless, she opened fire two minutes later, range 19,400 yards. ". . . more than one or two ships were rarely visible . . . consequently it was necessary to shift [fire] from ship to ship as they emerged from the smoke." The *Massachusetts* was shooting first at destroyers and then at the French light cruiser *Primauguet*, which joined the battle at 0900. The battleship noted return fire at 0921 and reported that enemy "fire control was excellent and numerous splashes of various colors were observed, many within 50 yards of various ships of this group."

Poor visibility and equipment failures affected American gunnery. The *Massachusetts* relied on optical spotting because the main battery director's Fire Control Radar 1 had blown a fuse, and Fire Control Radar 2's ranges varied so greatly from optical spots that the gunners discounted its output. At 0930 the concussion from a main battery salvo jumped a circuit breaker and all four FD Mk 4 and FC Mk 3 radars lost power "with a consequent loss of target pips." "Shooting was 'from the hip' with application of spots in range and deflection when salvo landed." Nonetheless, the French situation was dire and, as the battleship and her attendant cruisers and destroyers closed, it grew worse. Rear Admiral Hewitt, who had General Patton pacing beside him anxious to get ashore, withdrew because it seemed Giffen had taken control and the French were retreating. However, at 0935, having reached a point ten miles north of Casablanca and just 11,500 yards

The *Massachusetts* received two significant hits during the action. A 155-mm round fired by the French light cruiser *Primauguet* ricocheted off battleship's starboard quarterdeck at 1057 and burst over a 20-mm mount, igniting small fires. This photograph shows the splinter damage that resulted. (USS *Massachusetts* Memorial Committee Inc.)

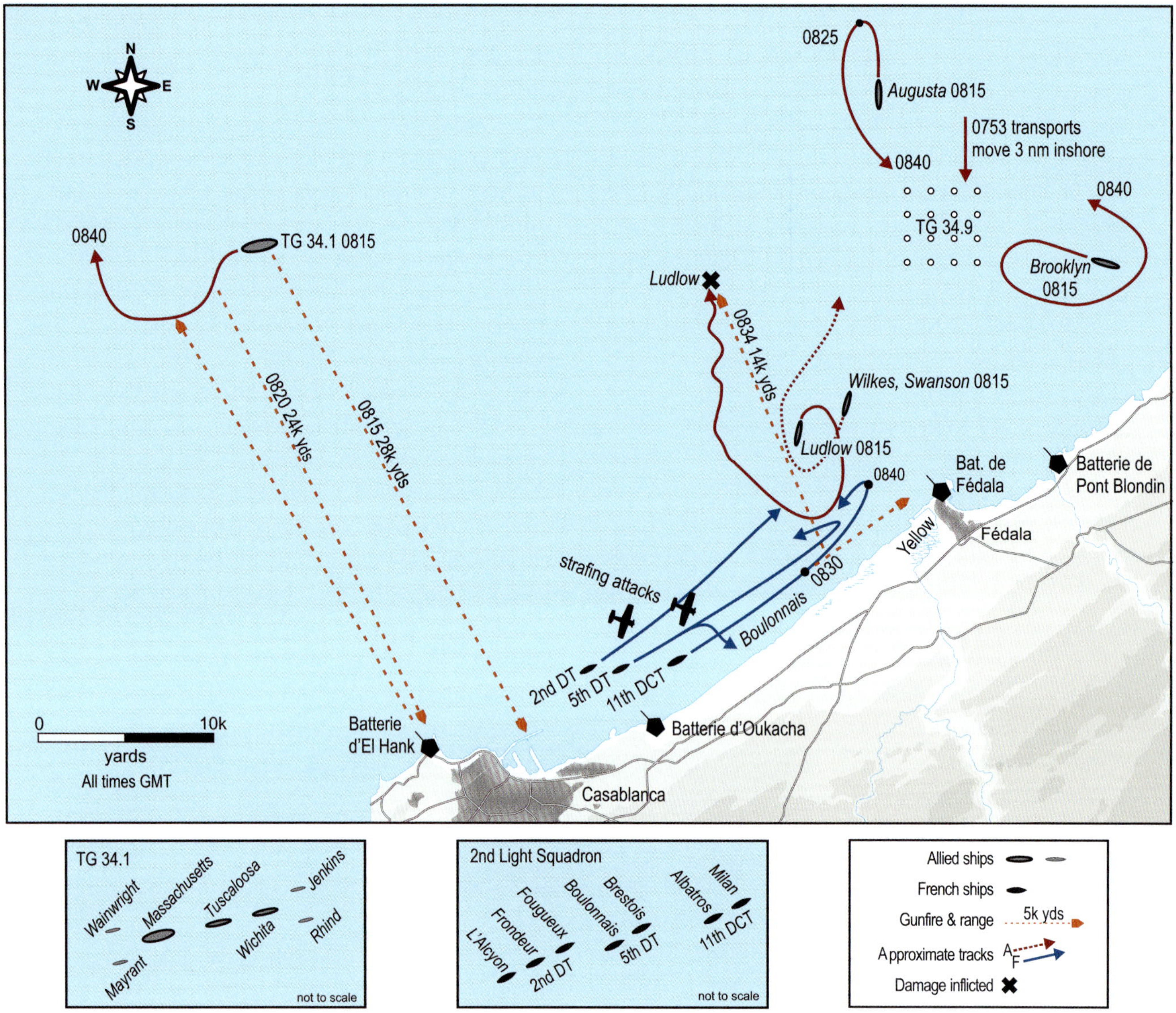

from the nearest enemy ship, the *Massachusetts* came about. The battleship's log records that this was done to avoid "restricted waters." Giffen's report only notes that "range varied from 11,500 yards at 0935 to 30,000 yards at 1016." This perplexing maneuver gave the *Primauguet* and the large destroyers another opportunity to make for the transports and now, with Hewitt's withdrawal, only destroyers opposed them.

As American destroyers assigned to supporting the landings skirmished with French warships northwest of Fédala, the *Massachusetts* steamed west, her aft turret engaging the *Fougueux*, *Frondeur*, and *L'Alcyon* to the south. At 0940 a 16-inch round fired from 12,000 yards crashed into the *Fougueux*. This, the first direct hit obtained by the Americans on the French flotilla, crumpled the destroyer's bow up to the quarterdeck, drove the stem underwater, and set the bridge on fire. The *Fougueux* rapidly flooded. Despite her radar difficulties and the poor visibility, the battleship scored again at 0956. The *Milan* was 2,700 yards north-northwest of Oukacha steaming southwest when she disappeared in a giant geyser. A 16-inch shell fired from 28,000 yards rumbled through the large destroyer, igniting fires and rupturing the hull. Splinters wreaked havoc and cut down more than a hundred men. This extraordinary blow was the longest-range hit obtained by one warship on another warship while under way during the entire war. The *Milan* turned into the wind to contain the flames and slowly drifted toward shore while survivors jettisoned ammunition and torpedoes. Because the *Massachusetts* continued to withdraw, however, the *Primauguet* and *Albatros* came about and headed back toward the transports.

As TG 34.1 passed to the north, El Hank opened an intense fire. Rear Admiral Giffen remarked that "there were many instances of enemy overs landing within 50 feet of the disengaged side, in some cases as close as 10 or 15 feet." The stately progress of the *Massachusetts* and her attendant cruisers across the battle zone also had attracted French submarines. One just missed the *Tuscaloosa*. Two sailors on the signal bridge simultaneously reported tracks off the cruiser's port bow, and the captain immediately ordered a hard turn to port. Minutes later the *Massachusetts* was 28,000 yards northwest of El Hank heading west at 27 knots when "a shower of wooden splinters so stunned [her] executive officer . . . that it took him a few seconds to realize the ship had been hit." One of the lookouts recorded, "you could see [the] shells and [one] went flashing by and down into the deck and exploded; it detonated in the Marine storage room, into all those nice, full dress Marine uniforms." In fact, a 194-mm projectile struck opposite No. 2 turret on the port side, penetrated a deck and detonated against the second, five-inch thick protective deck gouging an inch-deep hole. The main deck planking caught fire. There were no casualties, although one sailor's "locker yielded thirty shell fragments varying from the size of a pea to that of a match box." Then the same officer, who was conning the battleship from a catwalk, spotted torpedo wakes. Overriding Captain Whiting's orders he turned the *Massachusetts*, seeking to maneuver between a spread of four torpedoes launched by the *Méduse* at 1003 from a range of 4,000 yards. One sailor recalled, "We made a turn and I know no battleship has probably ever listed that much. We had things like the chief engineer's director's chair sliding down across those checker plates and the rag hands sliding across the checker plates and everyone's holding on to keep from sliding across the checker plates. We said what's going on topside because we didn't know and the guy who was on the phones up on the smoke watch, called down and said that three torpedoes passed on one side and one passed on the other side." Another sailor identified this as his most frightening moment in three years of war. "I was on watch in #2 boiler room. Now that's about frame 29 on the configuration of the ship. Well, right over the intercom, it says, 'standby to receive a torpedo on frame 26' and everybody froze, but thanks to the quartermaster, it didn't hit us." This torpedo reportedly passed five yards down the battleship's starboard side.

In 100 minutes of action the French warships had circled between Casablanca and Cape Fédala. They had moderately damaged the *Ludlow* and foiled a minor landing but had failed to seize two opportunities to attack the transports. They had been subjected to sustained fire from a vastly superior naval force as well as dive-bombing and strafing attacks. Nonetheless, with the effective use of smoke they had suffered the loss of only the *Fougueux*, the crippling of the *Milan*, and

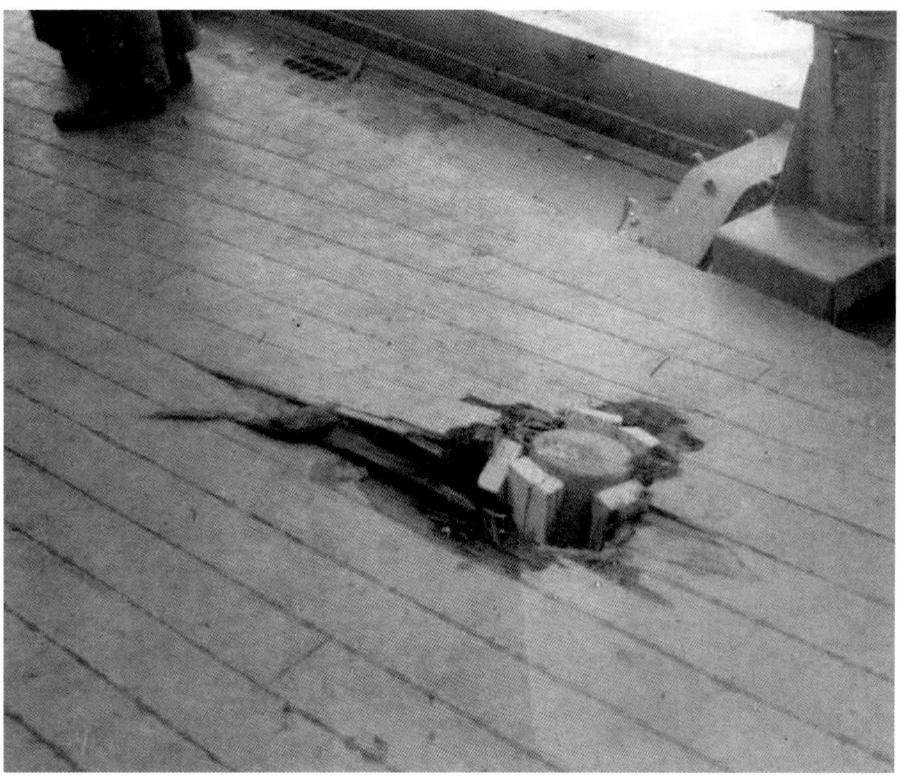

Massachusetts **was 28,000 yards northwest of El Hank when she took a 194-mm round fired by the battery. This struck opposite No. 2 turret on the port side, penetrated a deck and detonated against the second, 5-inch thick protective deck gouging an inch-deep hole. The main deck planking caught fire. (USS *Massachusetts* Memorial Committee Inc.)**

The U.S. Navy's ability to refuel smaller warships from larger ones while under way was critical to the Navy's ability to project power over oceanic distances, as in Operation Torch. Here the *Massachusetts* is refueling the *Gleaves*-class destroyer USS *Hambleton* (DD-455) on the day before the landings. *Hambleton* was torpedoed and severely damaged by *U-173* on 11 November. She was patched up in Casablanca and went on to participate in the Normandy and Okinawa invasions. (USS *Massachusetts* Memorial Committee Inc.)

moderate damage to the *Frondeur*. One cruiser, one large destroyer, and three fleet destroyers remained effective.

By 1000 Hewitt had returned to supporting transports and Giffen to his duel with El Hank. Giffen wrote: "It is believed that severe losses were suffered by the enemy during this phase." In fact, both admirals exaggerated the damage caused by their gunnery. This was understandable; it was their first surface combat and spotters and lookouts tended to see a hit in every puff of smoke, or ships rolling over and bows projecting from the water. Consequently, they embraced victory prematurely. Moreover, in just two and a half hours of combat the battleship had expended 580 16-inch rounds. There was another French battleship, the *Richelieu*, stationed 1,500 miles down the coast at Dakar, and Rear Admiral Giffen wanted to preserve ammunition in the (very unlikely) event the *Richelieu*'s squadron suddenly should appear.

The French admiral, on the other hand, refused to embrace defeat. By prolonging the action he gave his potential equalizers—shore batteries and submarines—opportunities to inflict a telling blow on the American force. The French remembered how, two years before, the British attack on Dakar had been foiled on the operation's third day when a submarine torpedoed the battleship *Resolution*. While the hope of repeating such a victory off Casablanca was slim, it was the second-best hope the French had. The best hope was to sink transports and at 1000, with the *Boulonnais* and *Brestois* forming up for an attack, the Americans were allowing French warships another opportunity to do exactly that.

The *Massachusetts* had vanished over the western horizon when the two destroyers appeared, nearing Fédala. At 0951 Hewitt once again had to interrupt his prime mission, which was supporting the landings. The *Brooklyn*, rushing to the action, barely dodged a spread of five torpedoes fired by the *Amazone*. At the same moment the *Boulonnais* and *Brestois* opened fire and straddled the light cruiser. The *Augusta* was north of the transports, refueling a plane and preparing to land Patton, but the general had to wait.

At 1010, an 8-inch shell plunged into the *Brestois*' forecastle. The *Wichita*, which was targeting "whichever of 3 DD's or *Primauguet* could best be seen in the smoke," likely was the source of this blow, which, if so, was delivered from near 27,000 yards. Two minutes later, the *Brooklyn*'s rapid-firing 6-inch guns staggered the *Boulonnais* with a crippling broadside that landed six shells on target. The *Boulonnais* shuddered to a stop and started to sink. Meanwhile, the *Primauguet* remained pressed against the coast zigzagging at high speed in an area 4,000 yards wide. The *Massachusetts* ceased fire at 1016 when she was 18 miles west-northwest of El Hank. She started back toward Casablanca at 1018. After nearly ten minutes her lookouts could observe "4 cruisers and 4 destroyers at the entrance to the harbor" with "2 cruisers badly afire." Big Mamie engaged this collection of French ships at 1030 from a range of 30,000 yards. She went to rapid fire five minutes later at a destroyer and claimed four hits even though her gunners complained of the smoke and difficulty in acquiring targets. In fact, she was shelling the immobile *Boulonnais*. At 1036 the *Albatros* tagged the *Brooklyn* on the No. 1 five-inch mount. The 138.6-mm round wounded five men before bouncing over the starboard side without exploding.

At 1052 the *Massachusetts*, steaming north-northwest at 27 knots with ranges to the *Primauguet* at 22,000 yards, reported shells splashing 25 yards off the starboard beam. As long-range salvos crisscrossed the smoky sky a plunging 155-mm round ricocheted off the battleship's starboard quarterdeck at 1057 and burst over a 20-mm mount igniting small fires. At 1103, after shooting 23 six- to nine-gun salvos over the previous half hour, the *Massachusetts* ceased fire. Giffen explained that the battleship "had expended 60% of her 16" ammunition and the preservation of the remainder was considered essential against a possible sortie of the *Richelieu*." At 1105 the *Augusta*'s guns also fell silent and she headed east toward the transports.

The *Boulonnais* sank by the stern at 1110, four miles northeast of the harbor entrance. At 1125 an 8-inch shell struck the *Frondeur* astern. She dropped out of formation with a heavy list and anchored at noon 1,800 meters off the port's entrance. At 1128 a round from El Hank punched through the *Wichita*, detonating on the starboard side and blowing a hole in the deck. It wounded 14 men, and fires filled several compartments with smoke and fumes. These were quickly extinguished

View looking forward from the ship's afterdeck during a lull in the Battle of Casablanca. Note: 16/45 guns of her after turret; 20-mm gun at left with "Lead, Dammit, Lead" printed on its shield; FC and FD radar antennas atop her gun directors; two large National Ensigns flying from her masts; and two destroyers screening ahead to port and starboard. (Collection of Rear Admiral Clifford Van Hook, 1972. U.S. Naval History and Heritage Command photograph)

and the ship's fighting ability remained intact.

By 1146 all ships had ceased fire, although the *Ranger*'s aircraft continued to harry the French, landing bombs on the *Primauguet*, *Brestois*, and *Albatros*. They so damaged the *Albatros* she had to limp toward the coast on one engine, and at 1155 anchored outside the port. The *Primauguet* and *Brestois* anchored nearby shortly thereafter. The *Milan* was still burning in the outer harbor, and the *Frondeur* was slowly flooding.

Task Force 34 had expended huge amounts of ammunition considering the operation was still in its first day. Hewitt had expected Giffen to contain the French flotilla, but fear of the *Richelieu* and a focus on El Hank had distracted TG 34.1 all day. For example, even though she had withdrawn from the surface battle to preserve ammunition should *Richelieu* appear, the *Massachusetts* exchanged fire with El Hank from 1345 to 1351, firing seven nine-gun salvos. The battery fired back, and as one participant recorded, "Every few seconds, intermingled between the shocking blast from our own guns, could be heard the ominous rumble of the approaching French shells and their sharp whine as they splashed a few feet on either side of the big ship or directly ahead or astern. . . . Why we were not hit dozens of times no one will ever know." Plainly running short on patience, Hewitt radioed Giffen again at 1340, "Light forces Casa Blanca making reported sorties. Destroy them before nightfall." Giffen sent the *Wichita* and *Tuscaloosa* to do the job, although their magazines were nearly depleted. In fact, the French fleet already was neutralized. After a dangerous long-range exchange with El Hank, the cruisers began opening range at 1450. With this the battle ended.

Throughout this long and confused action, the *Massachusetts* expended 798 16-inch rounds. She was hit twice with minor consequences, and a third shell passed through her battle ensign. The blast effect of her own guns caused far more trouble than enemy fire. Her after-action report listed the damage: "Heavy steel fixtures were torn loose from their fastenings . . . Steel doors in some cases stood swinging idly on their hinges, bent and useless."

Generally shooting at ranges beyond 15,000 yards and hampered by the enemy's use of smoke, the *Massachusetts* nonetheless disabled the *Jean Bart*'s sole turret early

Casablanca Harbor after the battle. The *Primauguet* is anchored top center left. The *Frondeur* (T-22) is capsized inside the harbor while the *Tempête* (T-52) is alongside. (U.S. Navy)

The transport fleet was anchored off Fedala, as seen here, waiting to unload when German submarines struck and, on 11 November, sank the large transport *Joseph Hewes*. The next day submarines picked off *Edward Rutledge, Hugh L. Scott*, and *Tasker H. Bliss* from the same fleet, accounting for nearly 54,000 gross tons of shipping over the two days. Not by coincidence, *Massachusetts* left for the United States that same day. (USS *Massachusetts* Memorial Committee Inc.)

in the action. She also sank the *Fougueux*, severely damaged the *Milan*, and hit the docked destroyer *Le Malin*. She turned in an impressive performance for a new ship in her first combat. The same was true of the cruisers and destroyers of Task Force 34. On the other hand, American tactics led to some needlessly dangerous moments. The U.S. task group commanders had conflicting priorities and failed to coordinate their activities. Hewitt had overall responsibility for all three landings, but the command arrangements put him in the middle of a battle on the bridge of a heavy cruiser while the army commander hovered impatiently at his side. The transport commander, even though he was on board a transport, had tactical responsibility for the *Augusta*, *Brooklyn*, and a destroyer division as shore bombardment vessels. He needed to secure the beachhead and get his transports unloaded, and his main concerns were the shore batteries, although that would have changed in a hurry had French destroyers burst through the smoke to confront him. Giffen was tasked with suppressing the *Jean Bart* and El Hank, watching for the *Richelieu*, and containing the French warships at Casablanca. These proved too many jobs. The fact that a battleship based 1,500 miles away received consideration while a French squadron sneaked out of port and attacked transports 15 miles away spoke to the deep respect battleships inspired in those with the job of potentially facing them, but reflected poorly on Giffen's sense of priority. Had the French warships reached the transports, had their submarines disabled the *Massachusetts* or one or more of the cruisers, the consequences could have materially affected the outcome of the landings.

On 12 November, once the landings had succeeded and an armistice was agreed upon, the *Massachusetts* turned back for the United States. The main danger in African waters was now German submarines, and against that threat the battleship was nothing more than a large and attractive target. Few ships received such a dangerous and important working-up period as the *Massachusetts* had in supporting Operation Torch. She acquitted herself remarkably well.

Her destination was the South Boston Naval Yard where she was taken in hand to repair defects and damage experienced in her brief but intense period of combat.

The *Massachusetts* remained in Boston until 11 December when she went to Casco Bay. The next day Robert Ogden Glover replaced Captain Whiting, who was promoted to rear admiral and sent to command Cruiser Division 14 in the Pacific. The month was a quiet one with training exercises on the 17th and the 22nd–23rd. On 29 December the *Massachusetts* returned to the Boston Navy Yard, in the words of her log, to "complete alterations and repairs to improve the military efficiency of the ship." On 5 January 1943 it was back to Casco Bay for more training and working up, and then on the 10th back to Boston where she "conducted such exercises and drills as Navy Yard work would permit." The work was tested with another run up to Casco Bay on 30 January. All the work proved satisfactory, and on 6 February, the *Massachusetts* raised anchor for what would be her longest voyage yet.

TO THE PACIFIC
March–October 1943

ON 6 FEBRUARY 1943 THE *MASSACHUSETTS*'S, ESCORTED BY THE *PHILIP* (DD-498), *Eaton* (DD-510), and *Renshaw* (DD-499), left Casco Bay for the last time and shaped course for Panama.

The first day out Big Mamie ran through heavy seas that tore off a gangway, caused a life raft to break away, and inflicted structural damage topside, but after that, she enjoyed smooth sailing at 18 knots on four boilers. She crossed the Tropic of Cancer on her third day out and arrived at Cristobal Harbor, Panama, on the afternoon of the 11th. One seaman remembered, "Then we got to Panama and everyone took off their shirts. We had about 350 guys with sunburns, but bad ones. I mean bad. One week you're freezing and the next week you're out in the

The *Massachusetts* seen from the afterdeck of the USS *Alabama* (BB-60), in Casco Bay, Maine, January 1943. The muzzles of the *Alabama* after 16/45 guns are in the foreground. (U.S. Navy)

The *Massachusetts* in transit through the Panama Canal. Her men, in dress whites, are lined up observing the tight squeeze as the ship moves through the lock with just inches to spare. (U.S. Navy Cruise Book)

beautiful sun." They passed the British aircraft *Victorious* on her way to the South Pacific as well. The *Massachusetts* serenaded the *Victorious* with "God Save the King" to which the carrier replied with "The Star-Spangled Banner."

After fueling, the *Massachusetts* began the tricky task of transiting the canal's locks—tricky because the width of the locks was 110 feet and the battleship's beam of 108.2 feet, less than a foot's clearance on either side. While clearing the Pedro Miguel Locks her starboard propeller caught on a safety chain, and the giant ship had to stop engines and go astern to clear the foul. She then continued on to Balboa where work parties repaired the damage. This allowed for a short period of shore leave. A sailor recalled that "they gave us one hour liberty in Balboa. They had about 300 guys that had captain's mast, being an hour late or a half hour late or something."

By the 15th the *Massachusetts* was under way for the South Pacific, escorted by the same trio of destroyers. Once at sea she conducted radar and rangefinder calibrations and drilled her antiaircraft and gun crews. On the morning of the 17th, for example, the ship expended 23 5-inch rounds, 899 20-mm rounds, and 240 rounds of 40-mm ammunition, firing at sleeves towed by her Kingfishers. That evening, according to the ship's log, "Davey Jones and messenger boarded the USS *Massachusetts*, emissaries of His Majesty King Neptune, to present His Majesty's compliments to the Captain, Officers, and Crew. They were very much displeased to find so many pollywogs on board. They informed the Captain that King Neptune and his Royal Party would board the ship at 00° 00' 00''." However, at the moment the battleship crossed the equator, the *Philip* was alongside taking on fuel oil. Work had priority, and even King Neptune had to wait. When the crossing ceremony did go forward, more than three quarters of the crew were pollywogs, that is sailors who had never crossed the equator. The pollywogs who got the worst of the initiation were those who had joined the ship after her return from Africa. One crewman recalled, "there were always a bunch of transfers on the ship and they were rough. They had the planes tow sleeve, you know. They threw all kinds of garbage in [the sleeves] and they had to go through there and they were beating them or hosing them down in there and everything, and then you gotta kiss the guy's belly and all that."

battleship, 1,400 nautical miles out from Balboa, provided 725 tons of fuel oil to her consorts in about five hours. On the 21st it was the *Massachusetts*'s turn, and between 0907 and 1258 she received 590,268 gallons of fuel (2,420 tons) from the oiler USS *Sepulga* (AO-20). On the 24th she dispensed 875 tons to the three destroyers, having come 2,800 nautical miles since the last fueling. The ability to routinely perform such a complicated maneuver was one other fleets lacked.

The *Massachusetts* refueling two of her escorting destroyers. One of the great strengths of the U.S. Navy in World War II was its ability to routinely refuel warships while under way. Note the turbulent waters between the ships. The ship's power and majesty also stand out in this image. (U.S. Navy Cruise Book)

One of the key elements of the U.S. Navy's ability to project power across oceanic spans was its ability to refuel ships while under way. The *Massachusetts* demonstrated this on the 18th after launching her three Kingfishers to patrol for submarines. The *Philip* came alongside at 1306. In less than two hours she received 55,713 gallons of fuel oil from the battleship. Simultaneously, the *Renshaw* received 63,059 gallons between 1325 and 1457. The *Eaton* got her share of 58,731 gallons between 1536 and 1711. Thus the

Major German warships could refuel from astern while under way but only from specially adapted tankers. The Japanese first tested underway replenishment during their voyage to Pearl Harbor in December 1941, and the British, except in extraordinary circumstances, did not practice underway replenishment until 1944. The battleships pursuing the *Bismarck* in 1941, for example, came near to breaking off the chase because they had to maintain a fuel reserve sufficient to get them back to base.

During her long transit, Big Mamie conducted gunnery drills and her Kingfishers swooped every day to make mock attacks. On 26 February her diary records that she carried out a "special exercise to determine arbitrary correction to hit for main battery, USS *Renshaw* acting as target, 16"/45 caliber battery firing 3 shot salvoes, 2 salvos at each range of 5,000, 10,000, 15,000, 20,000, and 25,000 yards."

On Thursday, 4 March, the *Massachusetts* was back in French territory, arriving at Noumea, New Caledonia. She had come 9,000 nautical miles from Maine in 26 days. This was roughly equivalent to the miles steamed by the ship from commissioning to her return from Operation Torch. By way of comparison, the Italian battleship *Vittorio Veneto* steamed 13,409 nautical miles during her entire career from June 1940 to September 1943, admittedly under far different conditions and under fuel restrictions such as the U.S. Navy scarcely could imagine.

At Noumea the *Massachusetts* was assigned to Task Force 64, consisting of the *Washington* (BB-56); flagship of Vice Admiral Willis Lee; *North Carolina* (BB-55); and *Indiana* (BB-58). After a few brief training cruises, on 7 April the *Massachusetts* finally got under way on her first Pacific combat mission, in company with the *Washington* and *Indiana*, escorting the large carrier *Saratoga* (CV-3) into the central Coral Sea. Nothing happened and the *Massachusetts* was back in Noumea by the 29th of the month. In May she ventured once again into the Coral Sea with the *Saratoga* and the battleships but again stayed more than 300 miles from enemy air bases. Lieutenant (j.g.) Douglas Butler, who joined Big Mamie in Noumea, remembered that "when I was notified the ship was coming in that day I checked out of the receiving station and went down to the waterfront and went to the pier . . . and so I had the thrill of watching this giant ship come into the harbor and tie up there to the pier in Noumea and then shortly after I went aboard and saluted the officer of the deck and told him I was reporting aboard for duty so they sent me around to the various places in the ship . . . My first impression of the *Massachusetts*: I was struck with the size and strength of the vessel."

June was spent at anchor, engaged in upkeep and training. On 27 June, Task Force 36.3, the *Saratoga* and *Victorious* protected by the *Massachusetts* (flagship of Rear Admiral Davis), *Indiana*, and *North Carolina* with the cruisers *San Diego* (CL-53) and *San Juan* (CL-54), and 13 destroyers proceeded north, once again into the Coral Sea, in support of Operation Cartwheel—the 30 June landings of the 43rd Infantry Division at New Georgia in the central Solomons. The *Saratoga/Massachusetts* group's assignment was to stand by in case the Japanese fleet at Truk intervened.

In conjunction with this operation, U.S. cruisers and destroyers fought three surface actions: Vila on 5 July, Kula Gulf on 5/6 July, and Kolombangara on 12/13 July. Vice Admiral William Halsey, the Navy's commander in the Southwest Pacific, rightfully held the fast battleships well away from these confused night melees in constricted waters. In fact, the *Massachusetts* never came closer than 240 miles to New Georgia. On 23 July Task Force 36.3 began heading south, and on the evening of Sunday the 25th the *Massachusetts* was moored in Noumea once again. On her three

Range and Endurance

A ship's range, that is the number of miles it could travel on one load of fuel, was a function of three things: fuel capacity, engine efficiency, and speed. In the 1930s, when the U.S. Navy began designing a new fleet to replace its World War I vessels, it identified Japan as its most likely enemy. It envisioned fighting across oceanic distances, so range and endurance were necessary qualities. The *Massachusetts's* range was 15,000 nautical miles at 15 knots or 10,610 nautical miles at 20 knots. She could carry 6,959 tons of oil as a normal load and more if required. In contrast, her foreign cousins had the following characteristics:

Class	Bunkerage	Range
King George V	3,770 tons	5,400 nm at 18 knots
Littorio	4,140 tons	4,580 nm at 16 knots
Yamato	6,300 tons	7,200 nm at 16 knots
Richelieu	6,796 tons	5,500 nm at 18 knots

Oil consumption increased dramatically as speed increased. As can be seen, however, the *Massachusetts* could go farther, faster than any of her foreign contemporaries.

major excursions into the Coral Sea the battleship had encountered nothing of the enemy—not even an air or submarine alert. On 1 August TF 36.3 was at sea once again with the *Saratoga* (but not the *Victorious*) making for Efate Island in the New Hebrides, which she entered on the afternoon of the 5th. There she remained for a week.

The *Massachusetts* stayed near Efate until 30 August when, as part of Task Force 38, she accompanied the *Saratoga* on another support mission toward the central Solomons, operating this time roughly 300 miles northeast by east of Guadalcanal. This excursion lasted until 5 September, when the task force returned to Efate. Through the end of October Big Mamie remained in the vicinity of Efate going to sea for training on 21–22 September, 7–10 October, and 20–21 October. The fast battleships were available should the Japanese fleet choose to intervene against the American offensive into the upper Solomons, but they were not needed otherwise. The dangers from mines and torpedoes were too great to risk the great ships in the narrow waters of the long island chain. In November, the U.S. Navy capped the drive by landing on Bougainville. By this time the United States, rightly dissatisfied by the time and blood spent conquering the Solomons, was looking to jump-start the advance toward Tokyo, still 3,000 miles away, with a leap into the Central Pacific.

Getting Under Way

The process of getting 40,000 tons of ship under way is much more than a matter of raising anchor. The ship's eight boilers generated the steam that was necessary to spin the turbines that provided motive power to the ship's shafts. Generally, one boiler would be kept lit when the ship was at anchor, providing steam to power the generators for electricity. The ship's diary for 12 August gives an idea of the process involved. "Boiler #5 steaming for auxiliary purposes . . . ready to get underway on 6 hours notice. 0347 Lighted fires under Boiler #6. 0443 Cut in Boiler #6 on main steam line. 0444 Secured Boiler #5. 0531 Lighted fires under Boiler #4. 0534 Lighted fires under Boiler #2. 0630 Cut in Boiler #7 on main steam line. 0635 Cut in boiler #4 on main steam line. 0655 Cut in Boiler #2 on main steam line. 0700 Made all preparations for getting underway. 0729 Underway."

A Kingfisher landing. This image shows the plane's crew arrangements with the wide separation between pilot and radioman. (U.S. Navy Cruise Book)

Vought-Sikorsky OS2U Kingfisher

The *Massachusetts* was equipped with three Vought-Sikorsky OS2U "Kingfisher" floatplanes. The aircraft handling arrangements consisted of two catapults upon which the aircraft were stored and from which they were launched. A crane positioned on the fantail lifted the aircraft from the water when they were being retrieved.

The Kingfisher was the U.S. Navy's primary ship-launched scout and observation aircraft during World War II. The first model flew in 1938 and over the course of the war more than 1,500 were built. The plane could carry two 100-pound bombs or two 325-pound depth charges. Its top speed was 165 mph and its range 800 miles. The ceiling was 13,000 feet. The pilot and a rear-facing gunner/radioman each had a .30-caliber machine gun. One of the ship's observers recalled that the aircraft was very rugged, a "good airplane but very slow. You were lucky to get over a hundred knots. It seemed like you weren't moving." As for being catapulted: "That was a thrill."

An aerial side view of three U.S. Navy OS2U Kingfisher observation-scout aircraft flying in formation. (U.S. Naval Institute Photo Archive)

Manning the ship

The full wartime complement of the *Massachusetts* was 2,354 men; in practice, however, this number was generally 10 percent less. The crew was organized into a hierarchal system designed, in the words of the Navy wartime publication *Seamanship*, to "implement the primary function of the ship—effectiveness in battle." The captain held ultimate authority over his ship and all that happened on board. His chief assistant was the executive officer. "He is thoroughly informed as to the policies of the Commanding Officer and sees that these are carried out by his subordinates in such a way as to insure the military and general efficiency of the ship." The entire ship's complement was organized into nine departments:

- Executive
- Navigation
- Gunnery
- Hull
- Communication
- Engineering
- Medical
- Supply
- Chaplain corps

Each department was headed by a commander or lieutenant commander. The ship was further subdivided into 28 divisions, one or more divisions in each of the nine departments. The numbers of crewmen assigned to each division that are given below should be considered approximate.

EXECUTIVE

The Executive Department consisted of the executive officer, the personnel officer, and two divisions:

- EX-1: in charge of personnel, correspondence, administration, and the band, with 31 men including the personnel officer, yeomen, buglers, photographers, and musicians.
- EX-2 (Police): with the chief master at arms and ten masters at arms.

NAVIGATION

The Navigation Department was headed by the navigator and had one division with 34 men including quartermasters, boatswain's mates, yeomen, and seamen.

Navigator works on charts in his office on bridge of USS *Yorktown* (CV-10). October 1943. (U.S. Naval Institute Photo Archive)

GUNNERY

The Gunnery Department was headed by the gunnery officer and had six gunnery divisions and four additional units: Combat Information Unit, Aviation Unit, Drone Unit, and the Marine Detachment:

Gunnery Divisions

- 01: approximately 130 men manning 16-inch turret 1 and including boatswain's mates, gunner's mates, turret captains, and seamen.
- 02: manning turret 2 and otherwise the same as Division 01.
- 03: manning turret 3 and otherwise the same as Division 01.
- 04: approximately 130 men manning the 12 quad 40-mm mounts and including boatswain's mates, gunner's mates, and seamen.
- 05: approximately 130 men manning the five twin 5-inch mounts on the starboard side.
- 06: manning the five twin 5-inch mounts on the port side and otherwise the same as Division 05.
- 07: Marine detachment with 80 men. They also manned 20-mm guns when at battle stations.
- TDD: with seven men, was in charge of the drone planes used to tow target sleeves.
- FA: with 50 men, was in charge of antiaircraft fire control.
- FM: with 65 men, was in charge of main battery fire control.
- CIU (Combat Information Unit): with 60 men by late 1944.
- L (Lookouts): with 65 men. They also manned 20-mm guns when at battle stations.
- V (Aviation Unit): with 20 men, included aviation machinist's mates, aviation radiomen, aviation ordnance men, and aerographers.

Crew levels fluctuated as additional weapons were added or capabilities, such as the combat information center, were refined and expanded. According to her quarterly personnel lists, the fewest number of enlisted men to man the ship was 1,817 on September 1943, and the most was 2,170 in the quarters ending on 30 September and 31 December 1944. To this should be added approximately 120 officers. The average number of crew throughout the battleship's career was 2,130 officers and men living in a completely self-contained world.

COMMUNICATION

The Communication Department was headed by the communications officer and had three divisions:

- **CR (Radio): with 66 men, including radiomen and radio technicians.**
- **CS (Signals): with 44 men, including signalmen and seamen.**
- **CY (Captain's office): with 23 men, including yeomen, printers, boatswain's mates, and seamen.**

HULL

The Hull Department was headed by the first lieutenant and had one division:

- **R (Repair): with approximately 90 men, including shipfitters, carpenter's mates, painters, boatswain's mates, patternmakers, sailmakers, and seamen.**

ENGINEERING

The Engineering Department was headed by the engineering officer and had four divisions:

- **A (Auxiliaries): with 82 men, including machinist's mates, water tenders, metalsmiths, molders, and firemen.**
- **E (Electrical): with 110 men, including electrician's mates and firemen.**
- **PA (Machinery space 1 and 2): with about 100 men, including machinist's mates, water tenders, boilermakers, and firemen.**
- **PF (Machinery space 3 and 4): the same as PA.**

Firemen man their stations in the fire room aboard the USS *Jouett* (DD-396). (U.S. Naval Institute Photo Archive)

MEDICAL

The Medical Department was headed by the medical officer and had one division:

- **H (hospital): with 35 men, including pharmacist's mates and hospital apprentices.**

SUPPLY

The Supply Department was headed by the supply officer and had three divisions:

- **S: with 85 men, including storekeepers, chief commissary stewards, ship's cooks, bakers, steward's mates, cooks, and stewards.**
- **SO: with 37 men.**
- **SS: with 35 men.**

CHAPLAIN CORPS

The Chaplain Corps consisted of a Roman Catholic priest and a Protestant minister.

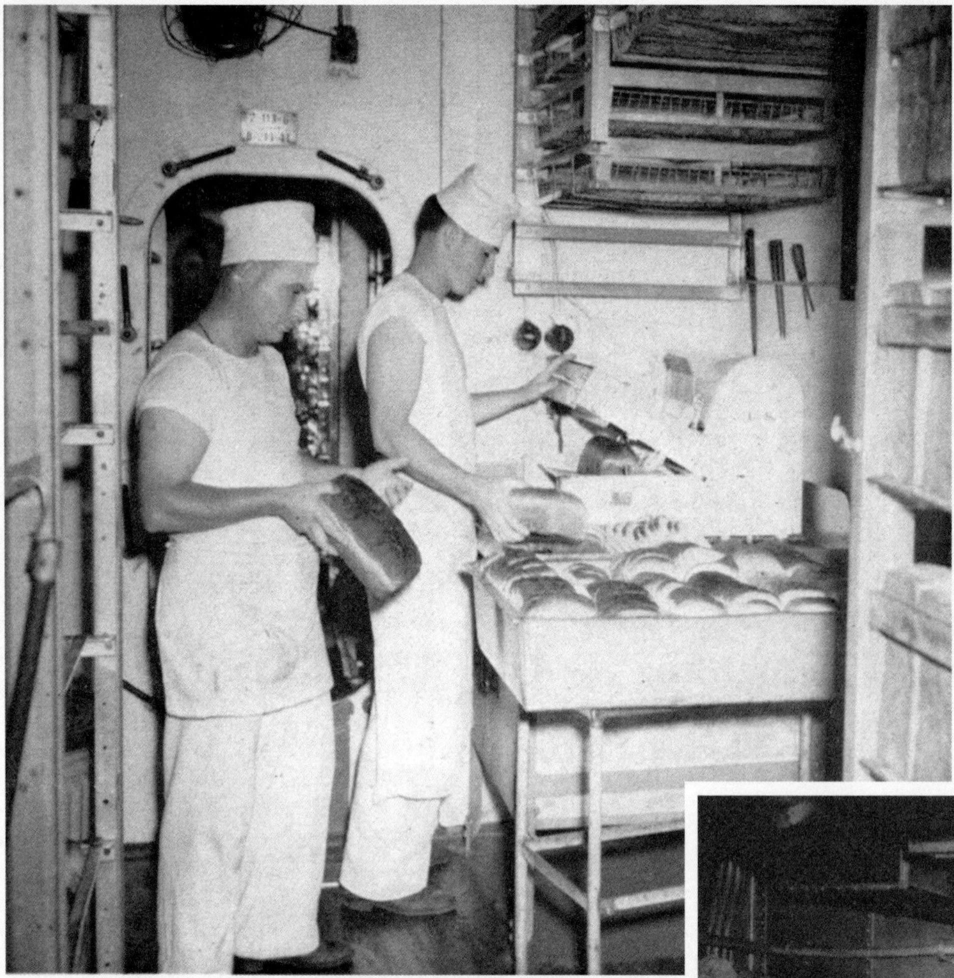

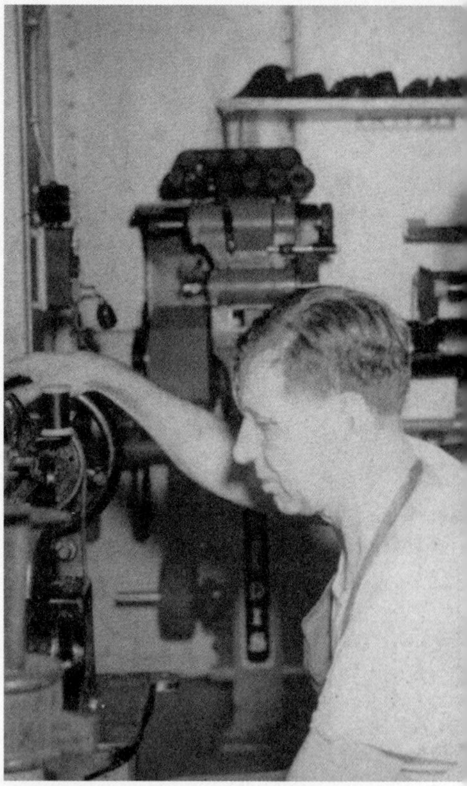

(top left) Ship's bakers inspecting a tray of freshly baked bread. The recipe for 300 biscuits called for 15 pounds of flour, 15 ounces of baking powder, three ounces of salt, nearly four pounds of shortening, and five quarts of milk. This was considered enough to feed 100 men. Thus, to serve the entire crew a portion of biscuits would require 300 pounds of flour and 26 gallons of milk. (U.S. Navy Cruise Book); (top right) The ship provided all the routine necessities of its crew. This is the ship's cobbler at work. (U.S. Navy Cruise Book); (bottom left) Three crewmen working in the ship's laundry. Their attire suggests a warm work environment. (U.S. Navy Cruise Book); (bottom right) The Machine Shop. Three jobs are under way in this photograph, with a hood or shield being fabricated (U.S. Navy Cruise Book)

The Daily Routine

The ship's day was organized into six four-hour watches. The first watch started at midnight and ran till 0400. The second was from 0400 to 0800, and so on. Generally, a crewman served one watch on duty and two off, although in times of danger or potential action the routine would be quickened to one watch on and one off, which made it difficult to get more than an hour or two of sleep in any one sitting. When at general quarters, the entire crew would be at battle stations. Moreover, when in enemy waters, the entire ship would go to general quarters during the half hours before and after dawn and before and after sunset, the reason being these were the times when the ship was most vulnerable and enemy aircraft were most likely to strike.

Every crew member had two stations: his duty station and his battle station. For example, a laundry man on duty would be a fireman when at battle stations. The Marines manned the 20-mm guns. Sailors who swabbed the deck while on duty were loading 16-inch projectiles in combat. As one sailor remembered, "You had to work. Ours was the 4th Division. We had the quarterdeck on the port side aft. . . . We scrubbed the decks down, cleaned and washed the bulkheads. They had something for you to do all the time. Get up in the morning, get a cup of coffee. Do a little washing the decks. Seven o'clock, go down for breakfast. Come back up about eight o'clock. Back on deck. Always something to be done. Clean this, clean that. It was monotonous . . . but when things got hot, it got pretty exciting." Another officer recalled, "An awful lot of free time, if you had any, was devoted to sleeping. I remember one time, I never went topside for over a week. It was just mainly going from the watch to the bunk and I never even looked out at the sea for an entire week." Or another officer: "In dangerous waters where we were going to dawn to dusk stand to and working four on and eight off, we were tired. And sleeping was something that took priority."

The *Massachusetts* at sunset. She is protected by an antitorpedo net. (U.S. Navy Cruise Book)

OPERATION GALVANIC: November–December 1943

ON 11 NOVEMBER 1943, THE 25TH ANNIVERSARY OF THE END OF WORLD War I, "the war to end all wars," the *Massachusetts* departed Nandi Bay, Fiji, to participate in Operation Galvanic, the invasion of the Gilbert Islands. The battleship flew the flag of Rear Admiral G. B. Davis, ComBatdiv 8, which included the *Indiana* and *North Carolina*. The screen consisted of the six destroyers of Desdiv 42. She sailed in company with Batdiv 6: the *Washington*, *Alabama*, and *South Dakota* and another six destroyers. Collectively, they formed Task Group 50.2.3.

From Operation Galvanic until the end of the war *Massachusetts* escorted the fast carriers as they supported a series of amphibious assaults. Here a bomb delivered by a Navy Grumman Avenger torpedo bomber drops toward a burning target on Makin Island during the first phase of the assault on the former British possession. The Japanese seized the Gilberts just days after Pearl Harbor. U.S. forces liberated Makin on 23 November 1943 after 72 hours of fighting. (U.S. Naval Institute Photo Archive)

The *Massachusetts* crossed the equator heading north on the 14th. Her diary does not mention any visits by King Neptune; presumably the ship had been purged of pollywogs. By that afternoon she was 30 miles west by north of Makin Atoll (Butaritari Island) in the Gilberts. She continued north, and the next day Task Group 50.2.3 rendezvoused 135 miles north of Makin with the nine carriers of Task Force 50, which had sailed from Pearl Harbor. Rear Admiral Charles Pownall in the *Yorktown* (CV-10) assumed tactical command. Task Force 50 then split into three groups, each based on a trio of aircraft carriers, to strike individual targets before the landings.

On 19 November TG 50.2, commanded by Rear Admiral A. W. Radford, with the carriers *Enterprise* (CV-6), *Belleau Wood* (CVL-24), and *Monterey* (CVL-26), Batdiv 8, and six destroyers operated 70 miles southeast of Makin while the carrier air groups repeatedly plastered the island. The battleships treaded water as the air strikes continued on the 20th in support of the 6,472 troops from the 27th Infantry Division that assaulted Makin starting at 0840 that day. Batdiv 8 did not have to concern itself with shore bombardment duties; the *Pennsylvania* (BB-38), *New Mexico* (BB-40), and *Mississippi* (BB-41) were on hand to take care of that, although with only 740 defenders, of whom maybe 300 were combat troops, the amount of force applied was surely excessive (in contrast with the famous and deadly landings on Tarawa that took place simultaneously to the south). Coincidentally, the *Leonard Wood*, one of the transports involved in the landing, had been with the *Massachusetts* a year earlier off Africa.

Rear Admiral Glenn Benson Davis, ComBatdiv 8. Davis spent many months on the bridge of the *Massachusetts*. He was an experienced battleship man, having been captain of the USS *Washington* (BB-56) and successfully fighting that ship at the Second Battle of Guadalcanal. He commanded BATDIV 8 from April 1943 through February 1945. (U.S. Navy Cruise Book)

Repeated reports of bogies disturbed the predawn hours of the 21st, but no attacks developed. At 0602 that morning a fighter shot down an Emily flying boat about ten miles from the force. On the 21st the *Massachusetts* refueled the *Boyd* (DD-544), *Brown* (DD-546), and *Bradford* (DD-545) as the fleet stood ready to defend against Japanese air strikes or a sortie by the Combined Fleet from Truk, a thousand miles to the west. On the 23rd the *Massachusetts* refueled from the oiler USS *Platte* (AO-24). The load of oil increased the ship's mean draft by 18 inches.

Multiple bandit reports enlivened sunset on the 24th. A squall was blowing up, and the *Massachusetts* maneuvered to stay within the bad weather. On the 25th flares started dropping around the battleship shortly after sunset as two dozen Japanese Bettys orbited the task group. The crew found this unnerving. "They would circle

Captain Robert Ogden Glover, center, being relieved by Captain Theodore Davis Ruddock Jr., in dark pants, on 27 September 1942. Ruddock had come from the Bureau of Ordnance; the *Massachusetts* was his first major command. Glover went on to command the 7th Fleet's Service Force as a rear admiral. (U.S. Navy Cruise Book)

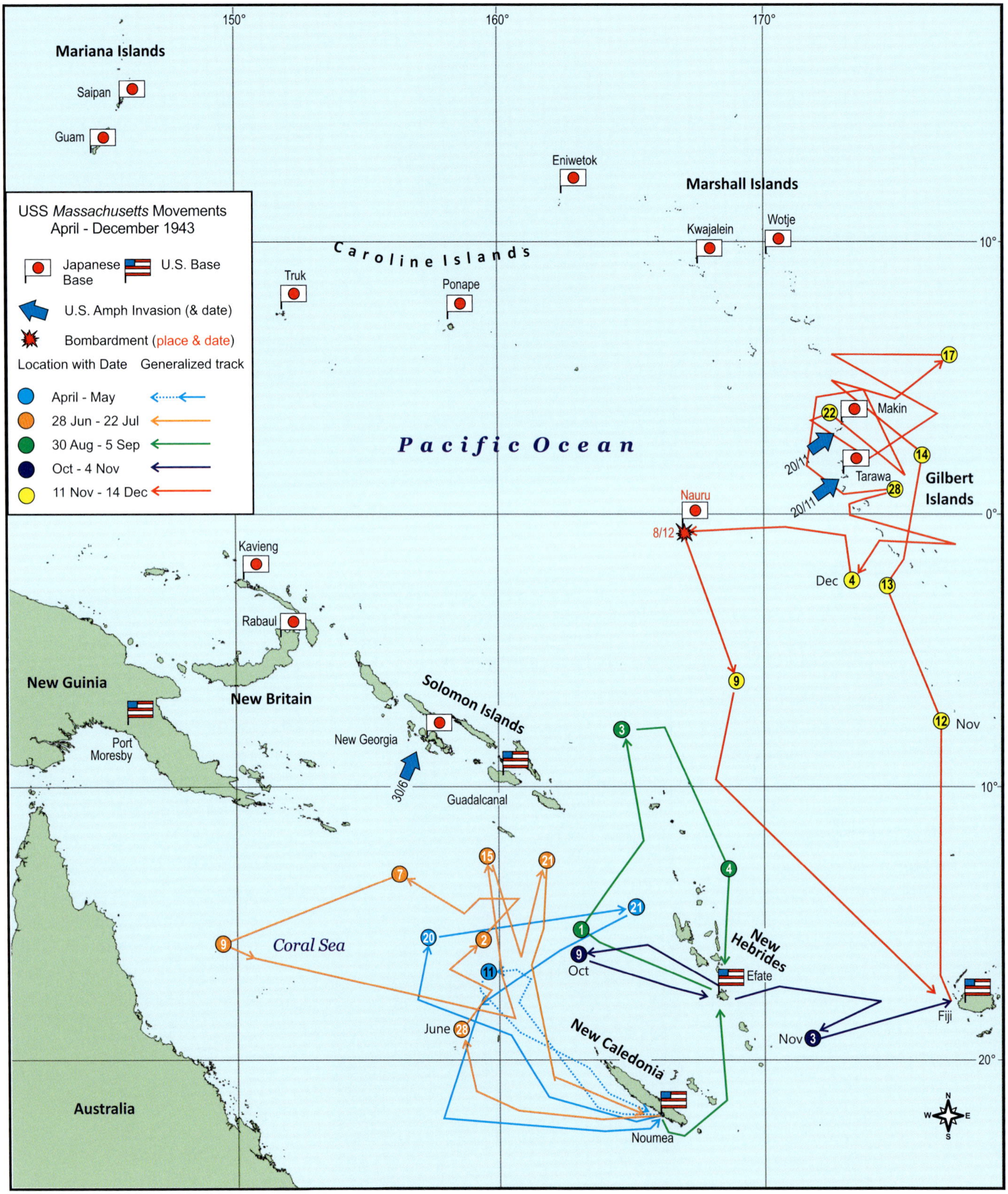

This chart shows the movements of the *Massachusetts* from the time of her arrival in New Caledonia in March 1943 through her return to Fiji on 14 December after Operation Galvanic. On this and subsequent charts the battleships' movements are indicated by colored lines with a different color for different operations. The circles show the noon-time position and the numbers inside the circles indicate the date. The month is generally clear from the context, but if not, it is indicated. The *Massachusetts* supported U.S. landings on New Georgia and in the Gilberts during this period and she bombarded Nauru on her way back to Fiji after the Gilbert landings.

around us and drop their flares, so they could see us. Most flares lasted too long; it seemed it was like it was hours before those damned things would go out." Another man remembered: "Just been aboard for a little while and they announced thirty-five planes coming in at us and I thought man, I just got out here and I'm gonna be killed already."

In fact, 18 minutes later a group made a "really determined approach" toward the *Massachusetts*. The battleship held fire until the raiders had closed to 4,000 yards, according to radar, and then her starboard 5-inch battery opened up. This was the first time since Africa, more than a year earlier, that Big Mamie had fired her guns in anger. The action lasted just 90 seconds, and she only expended 18 rounds. Nonetheless, lookouts reported that "a plane crashed off the ship's starboard quarter with its tail sticking up out of the water." The 40-mm guns held fire because they lacked radar control, and Captain Ruddick was concerned that if he used the 20-mm battery the flashes would merely illuminate the ship and make her an easier target.

Japanese Night Air Attacks. From Morison, *Aleutians, Gilberts and Marshalls*

"A little before sunset, one or more snoopers trailed the formation, waiting for darkness when they dropped a string of float lights marking the direction from which the striking planes would approach. These lights also served to mark the point of rendezvous. When the striking planes arrived, the snooper flew ahead of them high over the ships and dropped bright parachute flares. As the target became illuminated, groups of three or four "Kates" or "Bettys" armed with torpedoes launched attacks from favorable positions, one after the other, over a period of 30 to 45 minutes. Japanese night tactics were economical, as they required no fighter escort, and they were far more effective than the German Luftwaffe's night attacks on Mediterranean convoys in the spring of 1944."

The next night the Japanese aircraft again gathered along the fringes of the task group. At 1907 the *Massachusetts* fired a 30-second barrage of 5-inch shells (30 shells in total) at an aircraft coming in "low and fast." The plane veered off, although the gunners claimed a possible hit. Then at 1920 the lookouts observed a torpedo passing on the port quarter, and the ship surged ahead at emergency flank speed. The 5-inch guns erupted flame and smoke, this time at 7,000 yards, and the batteries expended 147 rounds over the course of 23 minutes, claiming one sure and one probable plane shot down. The battleship's report noted that "The attacks on night of 26 November 1943 were made by an estimated 20 to 30 planes. These attacks were much more vigorously made than the previous evening and appeared to have been well planned, though not executed with great coordination." Three night fighters from the *Enterprise* were one reason the Japanese attack lacked coordination. They harried the enemy, but lost one aircraft in the process.

A TBF Avenger flying antisubmarine and combat air patrol over columns of transports. This gives a good image of how convoys were arranged in columns and the spacing of individual vessels. (U.S. Naval Institute Photo Archive)

The Japanese deployed 27 aircraft, including six fighters and 17 bombers out of Roi, on the evening of 25 November. They named the engagement the Second Air Battle off the Gilbert Islands and claimed the destruction of an aircraft carrier for the loss of two bombers. The affair the next night earned the name of the Third Air Battle off the Gilbert Islands. It involved 31 bombers from Roi and claimed the destruction of two aircraft carriers and one cruiser at the cost of eight aircraft.

Japanese submarines presented another threat to the American forces attacking the Gilberts. Ten submarines had hurried to the area in response to the invasion, and two days earlier *I-175* had registered a major success when she sank the carrier *Liscome Bay* (CVE-56), which exploded and sank with the loss of 644 men. This tragedy confirmed that the longer amphibious forces stay tied to a beachhead, the greater the risk they ran. It was the same lesson the Germans taught the Americans off Morocco when their U-boats, arriving after the landings, sank five large transports. At 2256, only an hour after securing from general quarters, the *Boyd*, one of *Massachusetts*'s screening tin cans, picked up a surface contact nearly ten miles away. Admiral Radford ordered her "to go get it." She closed the target and, according to radar, surprised the submarine on the surface although haze defeated her attempt to illuminate. When the radar pip disappeared, the *Boyd* dropped several depth charge barrages at 0006 on the 27th and another at 0016 in response to "an excellent sound contact." After losing contact the *Boyd* remained in the area until dawn, when carrier planes joined to assist in the search. They found an oil slick 15 miles from the point of attack but nothing else. The *Boyd*'s captain, Lieutenant Commander U. S. G. Sharp, concluded there was no evidence of a kill "but it seems certain that the submarine was damaged." In fact, he had sunk the Japanese submarine *I-39*, probably in his second attack. In addition to *I-39*, the Japanese lost *I-17*, *-19*, *-21*, *-35*, and *-40*, as well as *RO-38*. The only survivors, *I-169*, *-174*, and *-175*, returned to Truk in December with slight damage from depth charge attacks. Task groups heavily defended by destroyers and aircraft were difficult and dangerous targets, and the isolated successes of Japanese submarines, as with the *Liscome Bay*, came at great cost.

A clear view of the arrangements of a typical breeches buoy. Notice the second line that pulls the pulley to the destination. (Hull Lifesaving Museum)

The fleet lay off the Gilberts protecting the recently conquered islands from Japanese counterattack until 1 December 1943. On that day the *Massachusetts* finally turned south with the *Indiana* and *North Carolina* and Desdiv 92 in Task Unit 50.2.5 to operate 300 miles south of Makin. That morning the *Massachusetts* lost a man overboard. The *Boyd* swung through the battleship's wake and within ten minutes had recovered the man and returned to station. Early that afternoon she came up on the starboard quarter and returned the man by breeches buoy, a process whereby a person transferred by rope between two ships via what today would be called a zip line. The routine back-and-forth cruising continued for several days, the tedium punctuated by false submarine alarms, the occasional sighting of a friendly aircraft, and by refueling on the 5th.

On 6 December Task Unit 50.2.5 was joined by Admiral Lee and Task Group 50.4. The two forces then formed a new Task Group, 50.8, consisting of BatDiv 6 (the *Washington* and *North*

Carolina), BatDiv 8 (the *Indiana* and *Massachusetts*), BatDiv 9 (the *South Dakota* and *Alabama*), the carriers *Bunker Hill* (CV-17) and *Monterey*, and a dozen destroyers of Destroyer Squadron 46 (Desron) and Desdiv 15. The purpose of this powerful aggregate of fast battleships was to dash 300 miles west and bombard the phosphate-producing island of Nauru.

Fast battleships in line preparing to bombard Nauru. Taken from a Bunker Hill aircraft. (U.S. Navy)

Smoke, haze, and a few burning fires on Nauru resulting from the battleship bombardment. Taken by a *Massachusetts* Kingfisher. (U.S. Navy)

The plan called for the carriers to launch strikes against the island and then provide cover against air and submarine threats while the fast battleships formed a line with the *Washington* in the lead and the *Massachusetts* fourth. At the appointed hour, 54 16-inch rifles simultaneously opened fire, sending 74 tons of explosives crashing onto the small island in one sudden and massive blast. As Captain Ruddock noted, "It is realized that the firing of this salvo without preliminary ranging shots probably will result in decreased accuracy. Its primary purpose, however, is to inflict the maximum casualties upon and generally to demoralize enemy personnel." After the first salvo, the *Massachusetts* followed with 29 more three- or six-gun salvos over 30 minutes. After a few minutes, her report noted, "impossible to see Island because of smoke. Fire on shore." She did have a Kingfisher overhead, however, and it reported her gunnery was "right on." The *Massachusetts* targeted the barracks area, the power house, gun emplacements, and supply dumps with her main battery and the airstrip with her secondary battery, expending 135 16-inch and 400 5-inch projectiles. Just at the time of cease-fire one of the carrier fighters looking for targets radioed, "Bombardment looks very effective. I can't see a God damn thing for the fire."

The only damage to American forces occurred when *Boyd* went to rescue an aviator downed two miles off the island. After sighting first an overturned life raft and then an object in the water that lookouts described as a man, she came to a dead stop 4,800 yards offshore, only to discover the object was a smoke float, not a man at all. Suddenly, Lieutenant Commander Sharp saw a flash on the beach and ordered both engines ahead flank, full right rudder. It was too late. At 1142 a shell slammed into the destroyer and exploded in No. 1 engine room, leaving a neat 6-inch hole and killing all personnel in the space except one man who escaped with serious burns. A second shell detonated inside the forward stack, and two shells barely missed. The Japanese battery unleashed a second four-gun salvo that registered two hits on the port side, peppering a large area with splinters, damaging two 5-inch mounts, and seriously wounding two men. The shells contained yellow dye, "which was sprayed over a considerable portion of the ship." As the *Boyd* accelerated and began chasing salvos, she tried to return fire but was embarrassed by a power failure caused by the first hit. It took a minute before the guns finally opened under manual control. Shifting to a standby supply power, however, remedied the problem, and the *Boyd* finished the action spitting shells in full automatic under director control. The Japanese straddled the destroyer five times before she drew out of range.

The American destroyer fired 306 rounds between ranges of 4,800 to 16,000 yards. The hole in her engine room caused significant flooding, and she was not able to plug it until 1808 after she came alongside the *Alabama.* As Lieutenant Commander Sharp dryly noted: "It is again apparent, as has been reported after other shore bombardments, that shore batteries are seldom permanently silenced by Naval gunfire. Considering the accuracy of the shore batteries fire, I believe that the ship was fortunate to come out with no more damage." Ten men died and nine were wounded in this action. The downed aviator was never found.

Even if the bombardment may not have been as effective as it seemed, the crew of the *Massachusetts* welcomed the opportunity to unleash on the Japanese some of the frustration created by their often dull but dangerous routine. Captain Ruddock wrote: "Although the use of these heavy ships for such a mission might be questioned, it is desired to point out that the action herein reported did more to raise the spirits of the crew of this ship than all the efforts put forth in other ways. . . . [T]he fact that firing was done at a Jap was enough to renew the men's feeling that they were actually in the war."

After the attack on Nauru the task group headed south, arriving at Havannah Harbor, Efate, New Hebrides, on 12 December. She remained at anchor for the balance of the year.

A 16-inch shell pattern taken by a Kingfisher. This off-target salvo was fired during the bombardment of Tarawa. (U.S. Navy Cruise Book)

A Bloody Proving Ground

The U.S. Fifth Fleet opened a significant new front in the Pacific War with the invasion of the Japanese-occupied Gilbert Islands in eastern Micronesia on 20 November 1943. Vice Admiral Raymond Spruance, commanding the fleet from the heavy cruiser USS *Indianapolis* (CA-35), launched Operation Galvanic with simultaneous amphibious assaults against Makin and Tarawa, two coral atolls lying 93 miles apart, slightly north of the equator. Tarawa, gateway to the fortified bomber strip on Betio Island, was the strategic prize. With Betio in U.S. hands, the airfield would bring the Marshall Islands, 550 miles to the west, within range of heavy bombers and reconnaissance aircraft of the Seventh Air Force.

The capture of Betio and Tarawa Atoll was the mission of the Southern Attack Force, commanded by Rear Admiral Harry Hill, and its landing force, the 25,000-man 2d Marine Division, commanded by Major General Julian Smith. Both men knew they faced a well-led, well-armed force of several thousand rikusentai, Japanese Special Naval Landing Forces. They also knew they would have to breech Betio's coral reef at low tide.

The proximity of the Japanese Combined Fleet in the eastern Carolines was a primary concern. Admiral Chester Nimitz, commander-in-chief of the Pacific Fleet, ordered Spruance to "get the hell in and get the hell out" to avoid getting trapped in shallow waters by an enemy counterattack. Timing also was critical. Nimitz grimly reminded Spruance that Tarawa represented a tough but brief stepping-stone for the pending campaign against the more strategically valuable Marshall Islands, slated to begin eight weeks later. The operational tempo was so taut that Spruance could not postpone D-day in the Gilberts even a week in order to gain a more favorable tidal range.

The hurried Betio landing would thus become a storming operation—a frontal assault against a heavily defended island in broad daylight during a dangerously low tide. Success would depend on surprise, simplicity, fire-support coordination, and speed of execution—difficult objectives to attain by even the most experienced amphibious forces. Very few ship captains or troop leaders in the Southern Attack Force had any previous experience in conducting an assault from the sea against a strongly defended beach. Tarawa would provide a bloody proving ground.

Artful surprise and sheer grit enabled the initial U.S. assault waves to gain a foothold on Betio's northwest shore on D-day morning, but the advantage proved temporary. Intense Japanese fire and a freakishly persistent low tide prevented the buildup of firepower and reinforcements ashore. Casualties mounted, communications failed, and chaos ruled the beachheads. The few fragmentary radio reports to reach Hill's flagship described stark conditions ashore. "Have landed," one message reported. "Unusually heavy opposition. Casualties 70 percent. Can't hold." Another message came from the epicenter of the fighting on Red Beach Two: "We need help; situation bad." Hill and Smith sent an urgent message to their common superior, Rear Admiral Richmond Kelly Turner, the Fifth Amphibious Force commander at sea near Makin, requesting commitment of the force reserve, the 6th Marines, to Betio, adding, "Issue in doubt."

The chilling words resonated throughout the chain of command. Desperate U.S. defenders of Wake Island, facing the Japanese landing on 23 December 1941, had signaled "Issue in doubt" in their final radio message. Alarmed, Turner authorized the return of the 6th Marines to the control of the 2d Marine Division.

There was more at stake for the Pacific Fleet in Operation Galvanic than possession of the Betio bomber strip. Defeat at Tarawa would derail indefinitely the promising new U.S. drive through the Central Pacific. Failure of the landing force to seize Betio Island also would discredit the unproven operational doctrine of forcible assault against strongly defended islands.

Tarawa after the landing. This photograph shows what a tremendous impact the sea and air bombardment could have on a target. (U.S. Naval Institute Photo Archive)

TARAWA IN THE PACIFIC WAR

The battle for Tarawa represented a crucial crossroads in the Pacific War. Twenty-three months had elapsed since Pearl Harbor; 17 since Midway. Although the Allies had seized the offensive from the Japanese in January 1943 with difficult victories at Guadalcanal in the Solomons and Buna, New Guinea, they experienced frustrating delays in generating their own offensive momentum. The Allies recaptured the Aleutians in 1943, but their subsequent amphibious campaigns bogged down in the thick jungles of New Georgia and Bougainville. The Japanese regional strongpoint at Rabaul, New Britain, continued to be an unassailable thorn in their side.

Marines on board a Navy transport study a relief map of Betio en route to the invasion. After months of relaxation and training in New Zealand, the Leathernecks were about to engage in one of the toughest island assaults of the Pacific war. (National Historical Center)

The senior officers responsible for waging war against Japan in 1943 faced serious limitations. The Allies had agreed from the beginning that the defeat of Adolf Hitler's Nazi Germany would constitute their primary strategic objective. Although the Combined (U.S. and British) Chiefs of Staff had postponed the long-anticipated cross-Channel assault against Fortress Europe until June 1944, preparations for Operation Overlord still demanded top priority for troops, planes, ships, and landing craft. The Pacific remained a backwater theater, whose few offensive campaigns had been limited in scope and scale.

Admiral Ernest King, representing the U.S. Navy on the Joint Chiefs of Staff (JCS), argued for greater offensive pressure against the Japanese by means of a second front through the Central Pacific. An outspoken advocate of sea power, King believed that the Central Pacific represented the royal road to Tokyo and the U.S. Navy should take the lead in such a maritime strategy. Yet King also insisted that the new front could be undertaken without drawing down European Theater assets by using the troops and shipping already available in the Pacific. At the Trident Conference in Washington in May, the Combined Chiefs accepted the U.S. "Strategic Plan for the Defeat of Japan," which included King's proposed Central Pacific drive.

The new strategy elicited different reactions from the two U.S. theater commanders in the Pacific. Admiral Nimitz, whose realm included enormous oceanic areas dotted with widely scattered small islands, welcomed the concept of his Pacific Fleet attacking west in parallel to General Douglas MacArthur's route through New Guinea and the Philippines. General MacArthur, whose South-West Pacific Area featured narrow seas and large islands, strongly opposed what he perceived to be a wasteful duplication of effort. He argued for a single, concentrated drive to the Philippines under his sole command, fully supported by nearby land-based air and, as needed, by Nimitz's Pacific Fleet. King, however, backed Nimitz, prompting MacArthur's strident warning that the Central Pacific's lack of advance fleet bases and airfields would result in catastrophic defeat—a "reverse Midway."

Proponents of the Central Pacific drive used the verb "whipsaw" to describe the effect of alternating offensives against the Japanese in the Southwest Pacific and the Central Pacific. In time, with MacArthur steadily advancing up the long coast of New Guinea toward the Philippines and Nimitz attacking through the Marshalls, Marianas, and Palaus, the whipsaw effect would prove its value. The alternating sequence of the U.S. landings at Bougainville, Tarawa, Cape Gloucester, and Kwajalein—within a period of exactly three months—proved the wisdom of this strategy.

Nimitz and Spruance believed that the Marshall Islands were too far away and too unknown to be the first objective of the Central Pacific campaign. Commanders of the 1942–43 landings at Guadalcanal, North Africa, and the Aleutians each had reported the critical need for advance aerial photography of the beaches and inland objectives. Taking advance aerial photos of remote objectives seemed a common-sense preliminary measure, but here, too, the vast Pacific posed vexing problems.

In 1943, existing aerial cameras were still too bulky to fit in carrier-based fighters. In fact, only a bomber the size of the four-engine B-24 Liberator had the capacity and range to collect aerial photographs in the Central Pacific. Seventh Air Force Liberators based in the Ellice Islands could reach the Gilberts, but not the Marshalls. Betio's bomber strip thus became the imperative objective. On 20 July the Joint Chiefs agreed to Nimitz's recommendation that the Gilberts supplant the Marshalls for the opening campaign.

The Joint Chiefs had other pressing concerns about the Central Pacific. Only a few islands in the vast region seemed suitable for airfields or fleet anchorages, and the Japanese, anticipating that any Allied advance would target such objectives, were busily fortifying them. In addition, the coral reefs surrounding most of these strategic islands further complicated amphibious campaign planning. There would be no "cake-walk" landings like those at Kiska or the Russells that had occurred earlier in the year.

Learning from early intelligence reports that the Japanese were fortifying Tarawa Atoll, the Joint Planning Staff advised the Joint Chiefs to undertake the Gilberts campaign with "battle-tested shock troops with amphibious training." Three U.S. divisions in the Pacific met these qualifications in late 1943: the 7th Army Division, veterans of the Aleutians and already earmarked for the Marshalls; and the 1st and 2d Marine Divisions, veterans of Guadalcanal, both currently under General MacArthur's command. With MacArthur preparing for a major amphibious assault of his own against New Britain barely a month after D-day at Tarawa, the JCS compromised, leaving the 1st Marine Division with MacArthur and transferring the 2d Marine Division to Nimitz for the Gilberts assault.

In preparation for the Gilberts, Nimitz chose Spruance to command the newly constituted Fifth Fleet and two countervailing firebrands, Admiral Kelly "Terrible" Turner and Marine Major General Holland "Howlin' Mad" Smith, to command the Fifth Amphibious Force and the expeditionary troops of the V Amphibious Corps, respectively.

LEAN AND FAT YEARS IN THE PACIFIC

The United States fought two wars in the Pacific, a consequence of the strategic priority accorded to the defeat of Germany combined with America's material unpreparedness to wage a two-ocean war in 1941. The first half of the Pacific War featured bare-bones resources, limited offensives, and hit-and-run raids, all conducted under the threat of the Japanese Combined Fleet. The second phase, beginning in late November 1943, finally reflected America's attainment of full wartime production, a tardy but awesome industrial transformation. One herald of this infusion of resources occurred with the arrival of the first Essex-class fleet carriers at Pearl Harbor.

Aircraft carriers were invaluable in the Pacific War. While vulnerable to land-based air attacks from nearby enemy airfields in the constricted waters of the Mediterranean and the North Sea, the carriers proved ideal for the vast expanses of the Pacific. Nimitz fought the first two years with no more than four carriers—sometimes as few as two—but in the war's second phase, the Pacific Fleet would include more than 100 flattops, many of them the highly capable *Essex*-class carriers.

Rear Admiral Charles Pownall would deploy six of these ships as the cutting edge of his Task Force 50 at Tarawa. Escorted by new high-speed battleships and logistic support ships, Pownall's carrier task forces could challenge the Japanese Combined Fleet for command of the seas. More than any other naval factor, the newly created Task Force 50 (soon to become Vice Admiral Marc Mitscher's Task Force 58) would make possible Spruance's stirring victories in the Gilberts, Marshalls, and Marianas.

ADAPTED FROM *NAVAL HISTORY*, DECEMBER 2008

RAIDS AND INVASIONS: January–May 1944

THE *MASSACHUSETTS* SPENT THREE WEEKS IN EFATE BEFORE weighing anchor on 18 January bound for Kwajalein Atoll in the Marshall Islands, via Funafuti in the Ellice Island Group. She sailed in company with five fast battleships and Desdiv 92 led by Rear Admiral Lee in the *Washington*.

The *Massachusetts* at anchor in solitary splendor at Efete. Two landing craft are visible to the left. (U.S. Navy Cruise Book)

On the 19th the battleships joined the carriers *Bunker Hill* and *Monterey* and four destroyers. The force anchored at Funafuti on the 20th and became Task Group 58.5. This represented the mightiest aggregation of battleship power gathered in the war to date with:

- Batdiv 6 (*Washington, North Carolina*)
- Batdiv 8 (*Indiana, Massachusetts*)
- Batdiv 9 (*South Dakota, Alabama*)
- Batdiv 7 (*Iowa* [BB-61], *New Jersey* [BB-62])

The *Bunker Hill* and *Monterey* formed a unit under Rear Admiral Fredrick C. Sherman; the three heavy cruisers *Chester* (CA-27), *Pensacola* (CA-24), and *Salt Lake City* (CA-25), made up another unit under Rear Admiral Ernest G. Small. Sixteen destroyers in four divisions completed the task group.

At Funafuti the *Massachusetts* took on fuel and 2,778 5-inch projectiles. On 23 January TG 58.5 steamed north and two days later met the rest of Task Force 58 three degrees south of the equator. This juncture occasioned another reorganization into four carrier task units. TG 58.1, built around the *Enterprise*, *Yorktown*, and *Belleau Wood* received the *Washington*, *Indiana*, and *Massachusetts* as its heavy support. These six capital ships were screened by just the light cruiser *Oakland* (CL-95), and nine destroyers. The officer in tactical command was Rear Admiral J. W. Reeves Jr. TG 58.1 continued north toward Kwajalein. Several submarine scares along the way proved to be false alarms.

By 29 January the task group was 40 miles southwest of Maloelap Atoll, the site of a Japanese air and sea plane base and a garrison of 3,000 men. TG 58.1's carriers raided the base at dawn, and during the day the battleships screened as the carriers launched and recovered aircraft. That night the force steamed east, and at dawn the next day the carriers struck Kwajalein Island. While this strike was under way the *Massachusetts* formed a line of battle with the *Indiana* and *Washington* while Desdiv 100 screened the capital ships. Their mission was to follow up the carrier strike with a bombardment of the island. Each battleship launched a spotter at 0910 as the line closed their target.

The *Massachusetts* opened fire on Kwajalein Island at 1015 from 11,000 yards. At 1019 a 5-inch battery on the island's western tip answered the battleship. The

The process of recovering an SOC. The ship has made a hard turn to port, creating an area of relatively calm water. The aircraft is coming on fast to hook up with the crane. There is a man signaling at the end of the catapult. Even though this is a routine evolution, it is interesting enough to draw a large crowd of spectators. (U.S. Navy Cruise Book)

This chart shows the movements of the *Massachusetts* from 18 January 1944, when she departed Efate for operations against the Marshall Islands, to 4 May 1944, when she returned to Majuro after operations off Hollandia, New Guinea. The range and speed of U.S. fleet operations are suggested by the vast distances the *Massachusetts* covered literally overnight.

first shells splashed 150 yards short. Between 1020 and 1024 the battery straddled the battleship's wake five times and the ship itself once. Five-inch mounts on all three battleships zeroed in on the imprudent battery and silenced it by 1039. The American attack also caught two Japanese cargo vessels and two small patrol boats in the lagoon. A rain of 5-inch shells from the destroyers and battleships quickly smothered and sank them.

At 1115, after 57 salvos, the battle line turned away to recover seaplanes. According to a fire control officer "firing during Phase I looked erratic—several splashes were seen falling short, while some also were seen to fall over." The battleships launched another spotter while carrier aircraft worked over the island during the break.

Phase II commenced at 1200. Over the course of a half hour, the *Massachusetts* flung 24 salvos at Ebeye Island. The observer remarked, "the 16-inch bombardment of Ebeye looked very good. The island was hit consistently during this part of Phase II." Another 60 salvos on Kwajalein followed up through 1344. The observer continued: "The Phase II bombardment of Kwajalein appeared much better than any of the previous 16-inch firing. All salvos seemed to be landing on the island." One caused what the spotter pilot described as the largest explosion of the bombardment. The battleship's rangefinder operator "snapped a range to the top of the 'umbrella' of smoke and measured it as 3,100 feet. *Massachusetts*'s secondary battery continued in action until 1455. The ship expended 362 16-inch and 1,902 5-inch projectiles throughout the day. Once again, smoke from explosions and fires complicated aim and made spotting a matter of guesswork.

The blast damage the *Massachusetts* suffered as a result of the bombardment alarmed Captain Ruddock. The ship had used reduced charges but it appeared the muzzle pressure from these was greater than the pressure developed by full charges with AP projectiles. More than twenty doors were sprung, broken, or completely blown off, causing "considerable damage to light bulkheads, staterooms, and fixtures within the superstructure." The repeated blast had torn off nearly two dozen vent ducts. Deck bolts worked loose, windows were broken, even the admiral's and captain's chairs sprang free of their bolts and were flung against a bulkhead. One of the SG radar sets went out for 15 minutes, but overall, radar proved more durable than at Casablanca.

The next day the air strikes continued while the *Mississippi* and *Pennsylvania*, with heavy cruisers and destroyers, pulverized the island. The landings went at dawn that day as elements of the 4th Marine Division attacked the northern islets of Namur and Roi, and the 7th Infantry Division assaulted Kwajalein itself.

After the landings a naval gunfire officer wrote: "The effect of naval gunfire on the island of Kwajalein was devastating. The entire island looked as if it had been picked up to 20,000 feet and then dropped. The

A massive explosion sparked by a 16-inch shell send an umbrella of smoke towering 3,100 feet into the sky over Kwajalein Atoll (U.S. Naval Institute Photo Archive)

The fast battleships firing on Kwajalein, taken from the *Massachusetts*. (U.S. Navy Cruise Book)

ground was so torn up that it made even movement by foot difficult . . . Prisoners of war testified that the terrific blasting effect of the heavy and continuous bombardment terrorized the defending forces."

TG 58.1 remained near Kwajalein with the battleships refueling on the night of 1 February. Even routine evolutions were dangerous. One of the ship's ensigns responsible for station keeping remembered: "You had a card which would tell you what the zigzag pattern was. It was very scary because you realized you got 25 or 30 ships out there and you're in the middle of them with aircraft carriers, battleships, cruisers, and a big ring of destroyers all around you and you had to be mighty careful because if you were a few seconds late or a few seconds too soon in giving the order you could get the whole formation into a really bad situation. And that happened." At 0419, with the task force zigzagging at 19 knots, the *Indiana* pulled out of formation to refuel three destroyers. In the process one ship zigged instead of zagging and the *Indiana* accidentally crossed the *Washington*'s bow; lookouts on the flagship did not spot the *Indiana* until the two behemoths were just 1,000 yards apart. Although the *Washington* went full astern and almost had stopped, she still rammed the *Indiana* on the starboard side abreast No. 3 Turret. The impact crumpled the *Washington*'s bow. The *Indiana* suffered major structural damage, and massive flooding

Eating in Action

During her bombardment of Kwajalein, the supply department issued the *Massachusetts*'s crew U.S. Army type "K" ration. According to the after action report, this proved "Highly satisfactory." The ration consisted of eight crackers with butter, a can of pork luncheon meat or processed cheese, a package of "Choclettos," four Chesterfield cigarettes (with matches), salt, a powdered beverage packet, and chewing gum. That sailors dining on this fare probably did not find it "highly satisfactory" is suggested by an account of soldiers

Breakfast version of K rations (U.S. Army Signal Corps)

living off the same rations: "They broke open their K-ration cartons, spread unseasoned potted meat on tasteless crackers and ate . . . in silence, not as one quietly savors a really delicious dinner, but because it was almost impossible to utter an intelligible sound with mouth filled with a substance which tasted like nothing so much as a cotton tablecloth." Indeed, one crewman remembered, "We had a tin can with emergency rations, but we never did get at those; that's for long term use against starvation because they were K rations, sealed up in thick waxy boxes and only broken out as an emergency and we never reached that type of emergency."

occurred on both ships. Escorted by four destroyers, they withdrew at six knots to Majuro for emergency repairs and then to Pearl Harbor. The *Washington* continued on to Puget Sound with a temporary bow. Both returned to service that spring.

On the 2nd the *North Carolina* and two destroyers joined the *Massachusetts* as TG 58.1 remained off Kwajalein. That day the 4th Marine Division overcame the enemy on Roi-Namur, but the Army's 7th Infantry Division required four days to defeat heavier resistance on Kwajalein. TG 58.1 then withdrew south toward Majuro. It was no longer needed off Kwajalein and frequent submarine alarms suggested danger there as there had been in the Gilberts.

TG 58.1 arrived at Majuro on the 4th and anchored in the lagoon. The *Massachusetts* took on 4,000 tons of fuel and 1,211 5-inch rounds and 31 16-inch projectiles. The Pacific command had accelerated the pace of operations to take advantage of perceived opportunities, so the fleet got under way once again on the 12th. The next objective was Eniwetok, 300 miles to the west of Kwajalein. This time the force consisted of Task Group 58.3:

- **Unit 5: Rear Admiral Sherman with the *Bunker Hill*, and the light carriers *Cowpens* (CVL-25), and *Monterey*.**
- **Unit 1: Rear Admiral Lee with the *Iowa* (flagship Batdiv 7): *New Jersey*, *Massachusetts* (flagship Batdiv 8), *North Carolina*, *South Dakota* (flagship Batdiv 9), and *Alabama*.**
- **Unit 2: Rear Admiral Robert C. Giffen with the *Minneapolis* (CA-36) and *New Orleans* (CA-32). Giffen had commanded Task Force 34.1 on the *Massachusetts* a year before off Casablanca. He had been disgraced off the Russell Islands in March 1943 when he lost the *Chicago* (CA-29) to a Japanese air attack, but now, after a stint ashore, he was back at sea in command of a cruiser division.**

Eleven destroyers of Desron 46 and Desdiv 15 screened the force. The ratio of one screening vessel for every capital ship showed how short the supply of destroyers was. Vice Admiral Raymond A. Spruance, in overall command, sailed on board the *New Jersey*. The plan was for the three fast carrier task groups to neutralize the Japanese base at Truk, which was within striking distance of Eniwetok.

On the 14th the Truk Striking Group had reached a point just 43 miles southwest of Eniwetok, and from there it turned toward Truk, steaming more than 500 miles to reach a point 75 miles northwest of the lagoon on the 16th. The carriers began launching strikes while Spruance formed a task unit consisting of the two *Iowa*-class ships, two heavy cruisers, and four destroyers to circle the atoll to hunt ships fleeing the air strikes.

The *Massachusetts*'s major contribution to the operation came at 1902 when she catapulted her two SOCs to rescue a downed *Cowpens* fighter pilot. Lieutenant C. C. Ainsworth landed in the lagoon, picked up the pilot, and took off again, being hoisted aboard just an hour after takeoff. Years later, his radioman, Dale Maudy recalled the rescue. "The first one we picked up he was shot down by an antiaircraft round that hit his propeller and he was going nowhere without a propeller so he landed in Truk lagoon and we landed and picked him up. I was with Ainsworth then. Ainsworth was the senior aviator. He was a great pilot and we were taking off in tremendous swells; I'd say 20-, 30-foot swells. We'd be sitting in the bottom of the swell and we'd look up at a 30-degree angle to the top of the swell coming toward us and, that's a frightening thing but then we'd ride up and bounce, take off for a few feet and then go down and land and then climb up again and we'd gradually frog hop and gradually get up to flying speed and then, we could fly then. Ainsworth was a great pilot."

The battleship avoided some air attacks delivered before dawn on the 19th and fueled that afternoon. Then, with Task Group 58.3 she started steaming north-

northeast for Operation Gateway, carrier strikes against Saipan in the Marianas. Japanese raids followed on the 21st after an enemy reconnaissance aircraft spotted the approaching American armada. The *Massachusetts* took credit for one aircraft shot down at the expense of 74 5-inch projectiles expended. Most of the Japanese effort, however, was directed against American carriers to the north.

On 22 February the task force sent three waves of bombers against Saipan. Following this lightning strike, TG 58.3 turned south. On the 27th the *Massachusetts* anchored at Majuro Atoll, the fleet's new advanced base. There she made further preparations for sea remaining at six hours' notice. Her diary noted that the captain granted "such recreation to the crew as is possible with facilities available."

The fleet spent three weeks resting and replenishing until 22 March when the *Massachusetts* got under way, once again as part of TF 58. The operation this time was Desecrate, a descent on Palau, Yap, and Wileai. The *Massachusetts* led the *North Carolina* in Batdiv 8, commanded by Rear Admiral Davis. Batdiv 9 included the *South Dakota* and *Alabama*. There also were three heavy cruisers and 14 destroyers.

Japanese aircraft spotted Task Force 58 en route and alerted Palau, giving fleet units based there time to withdraw. That day the *Massachusetts* was assigned to TF 58.3, which included the carriers *Yorktown*,

Shore Leave

One crew member speaking of shore leave said, "They'd give us cases of beer and food. The beer was very, very weak. We used to play baseball or tripball or whatever and sit around and just talk and drink beer and have hot dogs and whatever, but that would only last three hours. Then back to the ship and duty. It'd be very hot. Terribly hot." Another man remembered, "There were two beers per man but some ended up with no beers and others with eight beers. On one occasion the liberty boat returned to the *Massachusetts* and there were so many men who couldn't make it up the ladder that they had to lower a cargo net and hoist the eight-beer-men onto deck."

Rest and recreation on the beach at Majuro Atoll. The temperature was consistent yearly with lows in the low 70s and highs in the mid-80s. It rained, on the average, two days out of three. (U.S. Navy)

Lexington, *Langley* (CVL-27), and *Princeton* (CVL-23). The battleships included Batdiv 8 and 9; five cruisers and 16 destroyers rounded out the force. The two other carrier groups included TG 58.1 with the *Enterprise*, *Belleau Wood*, and *Cowpens*, and TG 58.2 with the *Bunker Hill*, *Hornet* (CV-12), *Monterey*, and *Cabot* (CVL-28).

The Japanese attacked the American fleet after dark on 29 March. The *Massachusetts* observed seven separate raids, but none presented "favorable targets for this vessel." Captain Ruddock noted that the only determined attack was made by three aircraft. Two were shot down in flames, and thereafter no aircraft closed nearer than 2,000 yards. The fleet suffered no harm that night. It was the crew's general impression that most of the enemy aircraft were not interested in attacking the battleship, and given her powerful array of antiaircraft weapons, this may have been true.

The smoke and flame emanating from a 16-inch salvo was a spectacular sight. The concussion was also dangerous both to the firing ship herself and her crew. Throughout the war the damage the *Massachusetts* suffered from the blast of her own guns was far greater than the damage inflicted by enemy action. (U.S. Navy Cruise Book)

On 30 March the three carrier task groups attacked Palau. Each launched six strikes starting at 0635. That night the Japanese retaliated with another series of raids. The *Massachusetts* expended 119 5-inch rounds against two groups of boogies, each time from 7,000 yards. She had to cease fire when other ships of the screen fouled her aim at roughly 3,000 yards. Again the fleet escaped unharmed. On the 31st TGs 58.2 and 58.3 hit Palau again while 58.1 attacked Yap. On 1 April all three groups struck Woleai. From there the combined task force headed south-southeast at 22 knots for a refueling rendezvous on the 2nd, 800 miles southeast of Palau. The task force then turned for Majuro Atoll. The weather was heavy on the 4th and 5th with frequent line squalls making air and antisubmarine patrols impossible. The *Massachusetts* entered the lagoon on 6 April, having covered nearly 2,300 miles since the strikes on the 31st. Not surprisingly, she replenished her depleted bunkers with 5,360 tons of fuel.

On 8 April the *Massachusetts* had a change of command as Captain William Walter Warlick, a past commander of Destroyer Squadron 7, relieved Captain Ruddock. Ruddock was promoted to rear admiral and assigned to command Batdiv4, flagship the *Colorado* (BB-45). Warlick did not have to wait long to see action. On 13 April the *Massachusetts* got under way as part of TG 58.3, with the same force composition as during the Palau operation. This time the mission was to support 7th Fleet operations against New Guinea, and a landing on Hollandia.

After a long but largely uneventful passage, keeping well away from Truk, TF 58 made a turn south for New Guinea on the night of the 20th. On 21 April TG 58.3 delivered air strikes against the Wakde Island air base off the coast of New Guinea west of Hollandia, having come 1,850 miles from Majuro. This was followed by attacks on the 22nd, 23rd, and 24th in support of the landings at Humboldt Bay. Army air force units already had pounded these targets, and there was little opposition; TF 58 was just churning mud. On the 25th, being advised that supporting air strikes were no longer required, TG 58.3 and TG 58.1 headed for a rendezvous with six tankers. On the 26th the fleet repeatedly scoped Japanese aircraft at a distance. On every occasion, fighters were vectored out to intercept them. Each time a Japanese plane was shot down, the fleet dispatched destroyers to rescue the survivors. They picked up five enemy aviators during the course of the day. On the 27th the formation headed east a degree or two north of the equator. It then took a sharp turn north for another crack at Truk. The *Massachusetts*, however, made a detour on the 28th in company with the destroyers *Converse* (DD-509) and

Thatcher (DD-514), stopping in Seeadler Harbor in the Admiralties. There Rear Admiral Davis transferred to the *Indiana*, which had returned to the fleet repaired after her collision with the *Washington*. Escorted by four destroyers, the two battleships then headed to rejoin the fast carrier group, something they accomplished on the morning of the 29th. The fast carriers raided Truk on the 30th.

On 1 May the *Massachusetts* with the *Iowa*, *New Jersey*, *North Carolina*, *Indiana*, *South Dakota*, *Alabama*, and 11 destroyers shelled Ponape for 70 minutes. During the first phase, lasting from 1530 to 1551, Big Mamie shot 45 projectiles in 20 salvos. Accuracy was marginal. Salvos 1, 5–9, 14, and 18 all hit in the water. In the next phase, from 1611 to 1629, she expended just 28 rounds in 15 salvos. Finally, the battleship engaged what aircraft had identified as 8-inch coastal guns. This phase commenced at 1637 and lasted until 1647. She discharged six main battery salvos using 14 shells and added 29 5-inch rounds. Any shore batteries present were wise enough to hold fire. There was a report of a submarine contact during the bombardment, however, and destroyers dropped depth charges in the battleship's vicinity.

After the action Captain Warlick remarked, "There were no occurrences of special interest during the bombardment. No enemy gunfire was observed . . . Such casualties as were experienced were minor and were promptly corrected except the failure of the forward Mark VIII radar, which took several hours to repair." TG 58.3 then shaped course for Majuro, where it arrived on 4 May. It had been an active period for the *Massachusetts* and the fast carriers she sailed with. Big Mamie, in fact, had been in active service for two years, and it was past time for refit. On 5 May she transferred 495 rounds of 5-inch ammunition to the *Iowa* and swapped planes with her, and the next day she set sail for Pearl Harbor in company with the carriers *Yorktown*, *Monterey*, and *Princeton* and the seven destroyers of Desron 6.

The force had a quiet five-day passage to Hawaii, arriving on the 11th. This was only a way station on her journey, and the hard-used battleship left the next day bound for Puget Sound Navy Yard at Bremerton, Washington.

Operation Hailstone

After the Gilberts fell, Nimitz prepared to move against the Marshall Islands. Convinced of the continued weakness of Japanese air power in the Central Pacific, the Pacific Fleet commander-in-chief brushed aside the fears of his principal commanders who favored a more cautious approach and aimed for the center of the enemy position—Kwajalein Atoll. Nimitz was proved correct when Kwajalein fell with remarkable ease.

To maintain momentum, it was decided to accelerate the planned invasion of Eniwetok Atoll, which was wanted as a staging base for advances into the Caroline and Mariana islands. With Truk situated 700 miles from Eniwetok, the vaunted Japanese base needed to be suppressed to prevent intervention.

Truk consisted of an enormous coral reef surrounding six principal islands and many islets, "a drowned mountain range inside a coral ring" as described by historian Samuel Eliot Morison. The reef was pierced by four openings covered by coastal defense guns. Hidden from world view, Truk had developed a reputation of nearly insurmountable strength. One air group commander would say, doubtless rhetorically, that his first impulse on learning the target was to jump overboard.

Fear of the unknown had magnified the threat, as Truk's reputation was greatly overblown. Only 10,000 to 12,000 Japanese soldiers and sailors garrisoned the atoll; also, Truk had just 40 antiaircraft guns, all of which lacked radar. But there was no shortage of aircraft. At the time of the raid, about 160 planes were ready for immediate deployment with another 180 ready for delivery to Rabaul and elsewhere.

The Truk raid, Operation Hailstone, would be conducted by the fast carriers of the U.S. 5th Fleet commanded by Vice Admiral Raymond A. Spruance, the victor at Midway. In January 1944, only weeks before the operation, Rear Admiral Marc A. Mitscher assumed command of the carriers, replacing Rear Admiral Charles A. Pownall, whose conduct of operations in the Marshalls was considered insufficiently aggressive by Nimitz's headquarters. Having grown up with naval aviation from its earliest days with service on board the Navy's first carrier, the *Langley* (CV-1), Mitscher enjoyed unequaled respect from the carrier commanders. They particularly appreciated his style of command, which was succinctly described by Mitscher: "I tell them what I want done. Not how!"

One of the few not pleased with the change was Spruance, who thought well of Pownall and resented his removal at the instigation of Vice Admiral John H. Towers, Nimitz's commander of naval air forces. Towers and Spruance clashed about how the carriers should be employed, with Towers' more aggressive outlook finally prevailing. Spruance would come to fully appreciate the talents of his new commander, judged by Morison to be *facile princeps* (easily first) of America's carrier leaders.

To develop information about Truk, two Marine PB4Y-1 Liberators flew 850 miles from Bougainville to photograph the base. Although clouds obscured the view, many warships and cargo vessels were observed in the lagoon. Admiral Mineichi Koga, successor to Admiral Isoroku Yamamoto, already had recognized Truk's vulnerability and had begun to withdraw the Combined Fleet. After the Marine planes were observed, this movement was accelerated and soon completed, with Koga himself departing with part of the fleet to Japan.

Rescue in Truk Lagoon. An SOC with three downed aviators perched on its wings. (U.S. Naval Institute Photo Archive)

Spruance's 5th Fleet included 12 carriers organized in four carrier groups. Expecting no important naval opposition at Eniwetok, just one carrier group was sent there. The other three groups, organized as TF 58, centered on five heavy carriers and four light carriers, headed for Truk. Hoping to engage Japanese vessels fleeing the lagoon, Spruance transferred his flag to the battleship *New Jersey* (BB-62) in preparation for a surface action. Since that hardly seemed necessary, Spruance's chief of staff wondered if his commander was essentially on a sightseeing trip, curious to see the base that had long dominated naval planning. Spruance's biographer, Thomas B. Buell, speculated that the admiral might have wanted to flaunt American naval dominance by sailing a victory lap outside the Japanese equivalent of Pearl Harbor.

The first success was scored the day before the raid when the American submarine *Skate* (SS-305) spotted and sank the light cruiser *Agano* as she left the lagoon. A Japanese destroyer saved most of the *Agano*'s crew, but nearly all of them would perish during the raid when their rescuer was sunk.

Sailing undetected to a point 90 miles east-northeast of Truk, TF 58 launched 72 F6F Hellcat fighters that arrived over Truk at 0800 on 17 February. Mitscher's strategy called for the Hellcats to fully engage the enemy fighters and soften up the ground defenses, clearing the way for the bombers. That idea worked perfectly, as 30 of the 80 A6M Zeros that rose were downed against the loss of just four Hellcats. After brushing the air opposition aside, the F6Fs headed for three principal airfields, where they destroyed about 40 planes. On the heels of the Hellcats, 18 TBF Avengers dropped incendiaries on the airfields.

One witness to the destruction was legendary Marine aviator Major Gregory "Pappy" Boyington, en route from Rabaul to captivity in Japan. Landing on Truk at the start of the attack, Boyington was hustled into a concrete slit trench as a Hellcat destroyed the aircraft in which he had arrived.

With Truk softened up, the attack on shipping began. Although the Combined Fleet was gone, the lagoon was crowded with ripe targets. Present were about 50 cargo ships and auxiliaries, delayed there because of weather, plus many naval escorts including three light cruisers and eight destroyers. Mitscher's fighters, dive bombers, and torpedo bombers carried out 30 strikes, each more powerful than those at Pearl Harbor. Air opposition was minor and sporadic, the only substantial resistance coming from antiaircraft fire.

When he received news that enemy ships were fleeing the lagoon, Spruance formed a task group centered on the *New Jersey* and *Iowa* (BB-61). With the admiral in tactical command, the ships circled Truk in search of prey, but with results that were hardly commensurate with the risks. A crippled cruiser and destroyer were dispatched, and two smaller naval vessels were engaged and sunk. In the process, a Japanese bomb nearly hit the *Iowa*, and torpedoes fired by the crippled destroyer straddled the *New Jersey*. Although an essentially cautious commander, Spruance was anything but that in needlessly exposing his capital ships at Truk.

That evening, the Japanese sent six radar-equipped B5N Kate torpedo planes against Mitscher's carriers. After being held off for about two hours, one Kate eluded the night fighter defense to deliver a torpedo that struck the *Intrepid* (CV-11). Eleven crewmen were killed and 17 wounded by the hit, which flooded several compartments and jammed the carrier's rudder. Withdrawing to Eniwetok under her own power, the *Intrepid* would be sidelined for several months.

Meanwhile, above the lagoon, 12 radar-equipped TBF-1C Avengers conducted the first nighttime bombing of shipping by U.S. carrier aircraft. Able to locate enemy ships in the darkness, the Avengers made 25 runs at masthead level, scoring 13 direct hits.

The onslaught continued after daylight. With light antiaircraft fire now the only opposition, attacks were directed primarily against airstrips, hangars, storage tanks, and ammunition dumps. Then, with Mitscher and Spruance concerned that the Japanese might repeat their success against the *Intrepid* if the warships remained after dark, TF 58 departed at noon on 18 February.

Spruance's raid cost 12 fighters, seven torpedo bombers, and six dive bombers, most lost to antiaircraft fire, plus the *Intrepid*'s damage and casualties. Twenty-two downed airmen were rescued thanks to efficient lifesaving efforts by submarines, destroyers, and aircraft. The price was minuscule in relation to the results.

Sixteen Japanese naval vessels were sunk, including three light cruisers, four destroyers, and nine auxiliary vessels; in addition, 19 cargo *marus* and 5 tankers were destroyed. In all, Japan lost nearly 200,000 tons of badly needed shipping. Still, Morison believed that with air opposition essentially absent, the score should have been higher. He traced the problem to overemphasis during pilot training on aircraft interception and amphibious support with too little attention to vessel attacks.

Of greatest consequence was the toll on Japanese aircraft. More than 250 planes were destroyed or damaged, leaving fewer than 100 intact. With his air defenses shattered, Koga recognized that he lacked the strength to defend the Central Pacific while the attrition of aircraft continued at Rabaul. Two days after Hailstorm, the Combined Fleet commander ordered his aircraft in the South Pacific to leave for Truk.

OPERATION HAILSTORM: FROM *NAVAL HISTORY*, FEBRUARY 2014

After the attacks on Truk, the fleet is steaming at speed to refuel and rearm. (U.S. Navy Cruise Book)

REFIT
May–August 1944

ACCOMPANIED BY TWO DESTROYERS, THE *MASSACHUSETTS* TRANSITED THE EASTERN PACIFIC FROM 12 TO 19 MAY.

The *Massachusetts* at anchor, view from the foredeck looking aft. (U.S. Navy Cruise Book)

Fresh from the yard, the *Massachusetts* is under way at 15 knots off Point Wilson, Washington, on 10 July 1944. (U.S. Navy)

She raised the coast of Washington State at 0342 on the 19th, passed the Tatoosh Light 90 minutes later, and anchored in Sinclair Inlet at the Bremerton Navy Yard at 1705. There the *Massachusetts* unloaded ammunition, completing the task by 0515 on the 20th. Afterward, she entered dry dock.

The process of getting the battleship ready for another deployment involved much more than scraping her keel and slapping on a new coat of paint. The crew enjoyed a welcome break from their routine. Most men received 20 days' leave; some were assigned temporarily to training schools, and only enough officers and crew to carry on yard work remained on board.

The refit process also included correcting defects, repairing accumulated damage, and making improvements and alterations as authorized by the commander of the Service Force, Pacific. There also were occasional setbacks. On 10 June a worker who was cutting through a bulkhead with a torch ignited a fire that smoldered for several hours, burning through the electrical insulation in the area.

On 25 June the ship emerged from dry dock and was moored to continue yard work and to complete her overhaul. The process continued through 4 July, when she undertook dock trials for main engines and auxiliary machinery.

The crew gathers at the rails for the first view of U.S. coast in a year, 19 May 1944. (U.S. Navy Cruise Book)

With the successful completion of trials, the crew started loading stores, which took five days. The U.S. Navy undertook the whole refitting process with a sense of extreme urgency, with shifts running 24 hours a day. On 0806 on 10 July, the *Massachusetts* was finally under way under her own power. She sailed into Puget Sound and commenced full-power trials, also firing 5-inch mount No. 9 to test its structural integrity. Next came high-speed tests of the steering control and rudders. At 1734 she anchored in Sinclair Inlet, and the crew started loading ammunition and more stores.

On 14 July the process was completed. The *Massachusetts* departed for the battle zone at 1108 with 76 yard workers still on board completing last-minute tasks. The crew spent the day calibrating the ship's degaussing equipment, determining the standard compass compensation, calibrating her radio direction finder, and receiving a draft of men for the 5th Amphibious Force for transport to the western Pacific. On the 15th, the workmen departed and Big Mamie was under way once again for Pearl Harbor, escorted by two destroyers.

The underway period was filled with drills and exercises and checking all the equipment, such as radar and fire control directors, to be sure they were working as required. All the guns were fired, and the escorting destroyers simulated torpedo attacks and helped the battleship conduct night combat exercises.

On 21 July the *Massachusetts* entered Pearl Harbor. There she embarked on a "limited availability period" to finish work not completed in Puget Sound. This phase lasted until 1 August when, in company of four destroyers, the *Massachusetts* set out for Eniwetok. A week of gunnery and tactical drills at sea followed as the ship steadily coursed west, reaching Eniwetok Atoll at noon on 8 August. There, in the words of her war diary entries for 10 August to 16 August 1944, she "anchored in Berth 423. Port War Watch is set, normal port routine being followed. Making all preparations for sea and maintaining a schedule of repair, maintenance and upkeep of equipment as permitted by Condition of Readiness for getting under way. Conducting routine training, drill, and recreation schedule." This schedule lasted until 31 August, when the *Massachusetts* entered the war once again, steaming out in company with Task Force 34.

Clockwise (all photos on this page, U.S. Navy Cruise Book): The *Massachusetts* in dry dock, her first destination after unloading ammunition and stores at Bremerton—she remained docked for a month and five days; slinging aboard stores and supplies for the next deployment, a process that seemed to attract a large audience of all ranks; Port of Seattle during the war. The city had a population of approximately 400,000 at the time, and the nearby port of Bremerton was, next to San Francisco, the most important naval yard on the West Coast.

WE SHALL RETURN:
September–December 1944

THE *MASSACHUSETTS*'S NEXT THRUST INTO JAPANESE-HELD WATERS kicked off on 31 August 1944, when she sailed as a part of TG 34.10: five fast battleships, Crudivs 14 and 13, and Desrons 52 and 50. They headed west along the equator practicing battle line maneuvers. As Captain Warlick told his men, "It is Admiral Halsey's hope that he can smoke out the Japanese fleet on one of these operations." As the carriers attacked Palau, the *New Jersey*, with Halsey on board, joined the battle line. They continued to practice tactical exercises through 9 September, keeping roughly 200 miles southeast of Palau while the carriers proceeded to hit Mindanao.

Puffs of smoke from exploding shells mark an antiaircraft barrage overhead as Japanese aircraft attack the fleet. (U.S. Navy Cruise Book)

On 11 September Halsey dissolved the battle line, and the *Massachusetts* was assigned to TG 38.3: the carriers *Essex*, *Lexington*, *Langley*, and *Princeton*, and the battleships *North Carolina*, *Washington*, *Indiana*, and *Alabama*. Crudiv 13 and Desrons 50 and 55 rounded out the force. On the 12th and 13th the carrier air groups raided targets in the central Philippines. The *Massachusetts* helped down a Japanese fighter that penetrated the screen and unsuccessfully bombed the *Princeton*. The strikes continued on the 14th. On that day one of the battleship's Kingfishers rescued a downed *Wasp* pilot. After recovering aircraft that evening, the task force headed southeast by south to keep a fueling rendezvous.

On 21 September TF 38 began launching fighter sweeps and air strikes on Japanese airfields, shipping, and shore installations around Manila Bay. Thereafter the weather deteriorated, and the *Massachusetts* refueled on the 23rd. On the 24th, with the target still the central Philippines, the battleship's Kingfisher rescued a *Princeton* pilot. Then, along with the *Alabama* and *Washington*, the *Massachusetts* joined TG 38.2 and headed for Saipan, where she anchored on the 28th. After one day in the Marianas the *Massachusetts*, *Alabama*, and *Washington*, along with the *Iowa* and *New Jersey*, weighed anchor for Ulithi.

The fleet reached Ulithi on the morning of 1 October. The next day Rear Admiral G. B. Davis, ComBatdiv 8, hoisted his flag on the *Massachusetts*. On the 3rd Big Mamie had to depart Ulithi on an emergency basis as a strong tropical storm blew up. The battleship successfully conned her way through the narrow channel using Mark 8 radars. She returned to Ulithi the next day after the weather moderated.

On the 6th the *Massachusetts* was under way as part of TG 38.3 with the *Essex*, *Lexington*, *Langley*, *Princeton*, *Washington*, *South Dakota*, *Alabama*, three cruisers, and Desrons 50 and 55; course 335 degree (true), speed 18 knots. The group's task was to support landings in Leyte Gulf by first striking airfields on Okinawa and Formosa, from which the Japanese could stage reinforcements, before turning against the Philippines. On the 10th, all four task groups of TF 38 united for the first time since June to launch massive raids on Okinawa's complex of airfields. As Captain Warlick informed his crew, "This new operation, as usual, will lead to a landing. When and where I cannot tell you until later. It is enough for us to know that Task Force 38 leads off, as usual, with a damaging blow to some important enemy position. The purpose of this blow is to weaken the enemy's ability to counter the landings when they come."

The arrival off Okinawa achieved tactical surprise; there were no enemy attacks the first day. The fleet then pivoted six degrees south the next day, as the ships fueled. The *Massachusetts* took on 458,041 gallons and dispensed 153,560 gallons to the destroyers *Healy* (DD-672) and *Laws* (DD-558). Then, with replenished bunkers, TF 38.3 ran in at 24 knots toward Formosa. The carriers launched planes on the 12th, but this time the Japanese were ready. Hundreds of fighters met the Americans in the skies over Formosa, and waves of bombers descended on TF 38. Little of this affected the *Massachusetts*. That evening, her antiaircraft batteries went into action just twice, as the Japanese did not

"A Display of Expert Seamanship." There appear to be three cruisers between the *Massachusetts* and the aircraft carrier in the background. (U.S. Navy Cruise Book)

press any attacks against TG 38.3. The 13th was a repetition. The *Massachusetts* went into action briefly at 1834, but the only American ship to suffer harm was the heavy cruiser USS *Canberra* (CA-70), part of TG 38.1. A Japanese aircraft from a specially trained night attack unit torpedoed her, and she had to be towed from the area. This necessitated a third day of fighter sweeps to help the crippled ship escape.

On 14 October Japanese aircraft torpedoed the light cruiser *Houston* (CL-81), part of the *Canberra*'s escort. On that day the fast carriers—except TG 38.1, which stayed to cover the cripples—turned southeast and withdrew at 24 knots. After dark a Jill, presumably from the Japanese TAF special attack force, penetrated the screen and dropped a torpedo at the *Langley*. The *Massachusetts* shot her down in flames a short distance off the starboard bow. A second Jill met the same fate. A third, however, crashed into the fantail of the cruiser *Reno* (CL-96), causing a few casualties and minor damage. After refueling on the 15th, TF 38 sent searchers north, believing the Japanese fleet was at sea.

At 1600 on the 16th, scouts reported a carrier and battleships far to the north, but a night search found nothing. That day Captain Warlick told the crew, "Admiral Halsey has made a change in plans for our Task Force. This change has been brought about by the enemy's reaction to our sustained strikes on Formosa, or rather it has been brought about by the enemy's opinion of the effectiveness of his counterattacks upon us. . . . The enemy apparently believes that he has sunk 53 of our ships, including 17 carriers. As we all know, that is all the carriers we brought along. . . . Two cruisers have been torpedoed, and are being towed out of the battle area. They are escorted by cruisers, destroyers and a carrier. It will be surprising if these cruisers and their escorts do not suffer additional damage during their retirement. They have fought off all attacks for two days. In the meantime our striking power is undiminished. . . . Admiral Halsey has moved Task Force 38 to a position where he can make a flank attack upon any enemy surface force leaving Japan to attack that group."

Rear Admiral G. B. Davis hoisted his flag on the *Massachusetts* on 1 October 1944. Here he is inspecting a division. Note the dark trousers and caps of the crewmen. (U.S. Navy Cruise Book)

Air Battle off Formosa - A Japanese Perspective

"The Battle off Formosa," by Vice Admiral Shigeru Fukudome, from U.S. Naval Institute *Proceedings*, December 1952 (78/21/598)

Immediately prior to the Battle off Formosa, we had an air raid by American carrier forces on Okinawa on October 10. On the previous day, October 9, one of our long-range patrol planes had disappeared far to the east of Okinawa. Except for that incident, we did not have a single indication of the enemy's approach. The attack on Okinawa was, therefore, a complete surprise. To make matters worse, we had stationed no planes on Okinawa at the time. We had not been fully prepared for launching counterattacks from Kyushu either. Consequently, we could not help sitting by as spectators to what was going on in the Ryukyu Islands.

Judging from the circumstances of the Okinawa air raid, we believed that the enemy would soon attack Formosa. On the 11th, for the first time, our scouting planes were successful in discovering the enemy carrier groups. Convinced that a major enemy air raid would be launched upon Formosa early on the morning of the 12th, I ordered my forces to complete all the following measures during the 11th, thus to be made ready for the impending battle.

October 12th dawned quietly, but at 0810 hours a radar station on the east coast of Formosa detected a great formation of enemy planes. This was the first wave of the enemy attack. All of our fighters took off from their bases at once; one group circled above Takao and the other above Taihoku to wait for and counterattack the enemy.

Although I was thoroughly aware of the manifest inferiority of our airmen's military skill as compared with that of the enemy flyers, I was confident that, as far as the defensive fighting in the air over Formosa was concerned, the odds would be in our favor at a six-to-four ratio. My confidence was based on two facts: First, we were able to use simultaneously as many as 230 fighters, a number which would, in all probability, exceed the number of planes the enemy carrier task force could dispatch at one time; and secondly, we were able to take advantage of our defensive position for counterattacking the invaders on our home ground. I expected that the foregoing two points would surely work in our favor, and that, therefore, no matter how superior the enemy flyers might be to our own men in military skill, there was no fear of our losing the fight.

What actually happened, however, was utterly contrary to what I had expected. As I watched from my command post, a terrific aerial combat began directly above my head. Our interceptors swooped down in great force at the invading enemy planes. Our planes appeared to do so well that I thought I could desire no better performance. In a matter of moments, one after the other, planes were seen falling down, enveloped in flames. "Well done! Well done! A tremendous success!" I clapped my hands. Alas! to my sudden disappointment, a closer watch revealed that all those shot down were our fighters, and all those proudly circling above our heads were enemy planes! Our fighters were nothing but so many eggs thrown at the stone wall of the indomitable enemy formation. In a brief one-sided encounter, the combat terminated in our total defeat. Looking up at the enemy planes which continued their perfect formation intact throughout the combat, I could not help heaving a deep sigh. It was a total surprise to me to see that, while our planes caught fire the instant they were hit, enemy planes, though momentarily smoking, did not catch fire, presumably because of their perfected fire-preventing devices.

Since our interceptors could not put up any real resistance, the enemy went on ravaging to his heart's content and inflicted terrific damage to our ground installations through strafing and bombing.

Though the number of fighters we lost in the first waves of the enemy attack was only about one-third of our strength, the real effect was much severer than the mere number suggests, since among those lost were many of the leader-planes. Consequently, when the second wave of the enemy assault came, as few as between 60 to 70 of our fighters in the aggregate throughout Formosa took to the air to meet the enemy. Worse still, none of them could offer resistance of any value. Finally, when the third wave came, none of our fighters could take to the air. In the meantime, our forces based in Kyushu unleashed a daring offensive against the enemy at sea. The offensive was launched on the 12th by 101 planes of the Second Air Fleet, utilizing Okinawa as a relay base. The sortie was made in a large formation in broad daylight and claimed, though dubiously, that two enemy carriers had been hit by bombing, with some damage. With reinforcement from the Third Fleet carrier squadrons, we repeated daylight formation sorties with about 400 planes on the 14th and with about 170 planes on the 15th. But the last two-day sortie claimed no perceivable result, with most of the planes having failed to sight the target.

It was the TAF (specially trained poor-weather attack force) alone which was credited with giving an appreciable blow to enemy surface forces. Beginning with the night attack on the 13th, the typhoon-trained air unit conducted sneak attacks on three successive nights until the night of the 15th. Each night about 30 planes were used. Immediately after the Battle off Formosa, Japanese Imperial General Headquarters announced that 12 enemy ships—cruisers and above—had been sunk and another 23 enemy ships had been otherwise destroyed. Most of this result was credited to the TAF.

THE EVALUATION OF THE BATTLE RESULT

As we have seen, the announced result of the Battle off Formosa was originated from the report by the TAF, which, under the command of Captain Kuno, was then based in Kyushu, away from my personal direction, though, as the Second Air Fleet commander, I was officially responsible for it.

After the war ended in 1945, I was told that of the ships in the U.S. Fleet only two cruisers had sustained serious damage. Why on earth had such an exorbitant exaggeration been made in our report? Having been informed of the real damage, I was startled indeed at the great discrepancy, nor can we shrink from the responsibility for having made such a report.

The losses on our part were really great. Against the surface units of the enemy carrier task forces, we made 761 sorties in all, and lost 179 planes in these sorties. In addition, we lost about 150 planes in the air and on the ground in Formosa. The damage to the military installations was also very severe. My original confidence in our ability to fight out the battle with six-to-four odds in our favor was shattered. The battle was fought with nine-to-one odds in favor of the enemy.

The results achieved by air forces were always exaggerated by airmen. As I have explained elsewhere, the TAF was the cream of my fleet strength and had been trained for night attack. I was convinced that such a trained unit could achieve one-third of what they claimed.

As a matter of fact, however, the real result they had obtained was less than one-tenth of what they claimed. The exaggerated report caused the Imperial General Headquarters to commit, though temporarily, a mistake in its estimate of the war situation. It made the nation indulge in a false celebration and created the illusion that the Empire could turn the tide of the war.

For my part I ascertained through the reconnaissance planes' report on the 16th that the damage done to the enemy was slight, and I was convinced that a major invasion of the Philippines would soon be launched. As soon as the Battle off Formosa was over, I made all haste in preparations for our move to the Philippine theater.

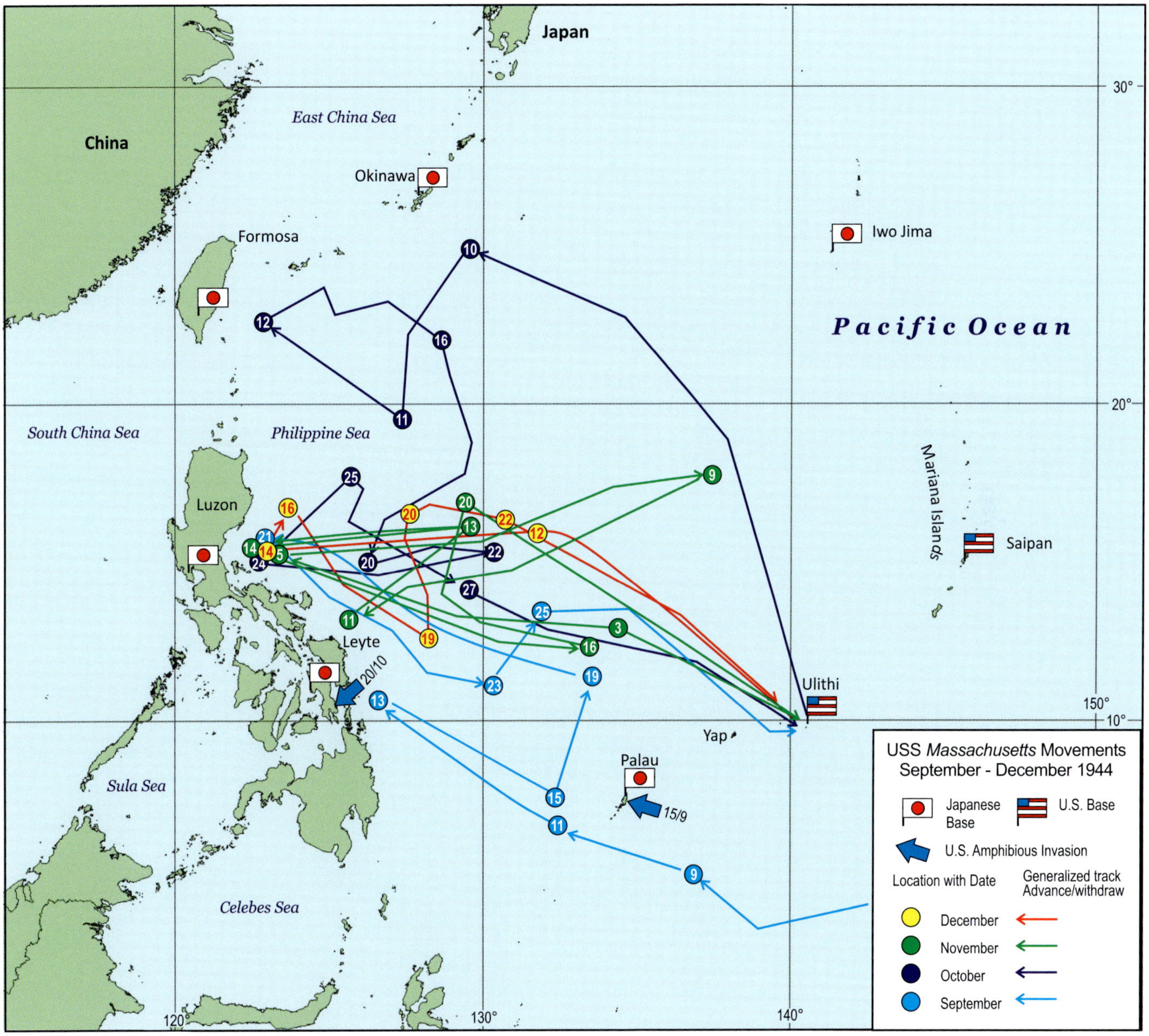

This chart shows the movements of the *Massachusetts* from September through December 1944. The major action during this period was the Battle of Leyte Gulf. The weblike density of the battleship's movements over a relatively short period stands as a testimony to the ability of the U.S. Navy to extract the most from its assets.

Although portions of TG 38 struck North Luzon and the Manila area over the next three days, the *Massachusetts* and TG 38.3 remained approximately 400 miles east of Manila, steaming in "strategic support of the Philippine Operations" and awaiting news that the Japanese fleet was at sea.

Four American divisions landed on Leyte on 20 October. TG 38.3 conducted air operations against the northern Visayas on the 21st, but generally it was careful to keep its bunkers topped and await developments. Early on 24 October reports arrived that as many as seven enemy battleships were approaching. TG 38.3's combat air patrol intercepted a Japanese air strike at 0755 that day, but at 0837 a second group penetrated the patrol and roughly 30 bogeys closed the task group. The light carrier *Princeton* was recovering aircraft. According to her report:

"The gasoline detail commenced fueling the planes which had just landed aboard. At 0912 the *Essex* had just reported a possible "bogey," together with a friendly plane . . . but there were no further reports by any ships of unidentified aircraft within a radius of about 25 miles of the formation." However, "At 0938 a single Japanese VB aircraft type 'Judy' was sighted by the *Princeton* lookouts diving on this vessel from out of the low cloud cover ahead of the ship. . . the enemy plane dropped a single bomb which scored a direct hit about 15 feet off the centerline to port."

At first the damage did not seem critical as the carrier returned to station and maintained speed, but in fact the bomb exploded between the main and second deck. The detonation ignited the fuel in six torpedo bombers in the hangar deck ("fitted with torpedoes and full auxiliary wing tanks in addition to

Smoke rises from an explosion in the *Princeton*'s hangar deck at 1000.5 hrs. on 24 October 1944, shortly after she was hit by a Japanese bomb while operating off the Philippines. (U.S. Navy)

The Battles of Leyte Gulf

[The Japanese plan] Sho-1 aspired to repulse the invasion of the Philippines by bringing the Imperial Navy's still-formidable surface action forces into contact with Kinkaid's amphibious units in Leyte Gulf. To execute this agenda, the Japanese reverted to the complicated tactics Spruance had anticipated at Philippine Sea. During the ensuing battle, U.S. forces referred to Japanese formations according to their relative positions. Northern Force, commanded by Vice Admiral Jisaburo Ozawa, consisted of the heavy carrier *Zuikaku*, three light carriers, two hybrid battleship-carriers, three cruisers, and eight destroyer types. Powerful as this force would appear from the air, it embarked only 116 planes. Its mission, expected to entail its annihilation, was to draw Halsey northward away from Leyte Gulf while two gunfire groups converged on Kinkaid. Center Force, the strongest Japanese formation, was commanded by Admiral Kurita. Composed of the superdreadnoughts *Musashi* and *Yamato*, three lesser battleships, 12 cruisers, and 15 destroyers, it would thrust through San Bernardino Strait to enter Leyte Gulf from the north. Southern Force was to transit Surigao Strait to enter the gulf from the south. It advanced in two echelons. The first, under Vice Admiral Shoji Nishimura, included two battleships, a cruiser, and four destroyers; the second, under Vice Admiral Kiyohide Shima, three cruisers and seven destroyers. Land-based naval aircraft in the Philippines were to support the operation

Early on 23 October submarines sighted and reported Center Force on its way toward the Philippines. The next morning U.S. air searches located Center Force and Southern Force, but, ironically, not Northern Force. While Kinkaid began concentrating his fighting ships at Surigao Strait, for which Southern Force was clearly bound, Halsey launched five strikes against Center Force as it pushed across the Sibuyan Sea. Although no Japanese ships were sunk in these attacks, the mighty *Musashi* sustained so many hits that she went down hours later, and at 1400 Halsey's pilots reported that Center Force had reversed course. In case it should double back, at 1512 Halsey issued a preparatory command detailing the composition of a battle line, Task Force 34, that, upon the order to execute, would be formed under Admiral Lee. Unfortunately, Admiral Kinkaid, whose communicators intercepted the signal, assumed that TF-34 had actually been called into being.

Throughout the day Halsey and the Third Fleet staff had puzzled over the apparent absence of carriers from the enemy order of battle. The mystery was solved around 1700, when they learned that aerial reconnaissance had discovered Northern Force off Cape Engano, the northeastern tip of Luzon, approximately 400 miles from Leyte Gulf. In contrast to the orders given Spruance before the invasion of the Marianas, which directed him only to "capture, occupy, and defend" specified islands, the operations plan issued to Halsey for Leyte included the stipulation that "In case opportunity for destruction of major portion of the enemy fleet offer [sic] or can be created, such destruction becomes primary task." At the moment, that opportunity seemed to beckon. For three hours Halsey and his staff considered their options. At 2000, convinced by aviators' reports that Center Force had been hurt too badly to inconvenience anyone, Halsey decided to take his entire force to attack the enemy carriers. The wording of the message announcing that decision left Kinkaid under the impression that TF-34 was guarding San Bernardino Strait.

Almost exactly three hours before Halsey began to move north, Kurita swung his Center Force back toward the east. Several U.S. air searches reported the Japanese advance between 1935 and 2320. This intelligence inspired some of Halsey's subordinates to conclude that Northern Force was indeed a decoy (a possibility his staff had weighed and rejected) and that part of TF-38 should remain behind to prevent Center Force from debouching through San Bernardino Strait.

An hour earlier, Nishimura had led Southern Force into Surigao Strait. Inside the strait, Kinkaid had extended a gauntlet of 39 patrol torpedo (PT) boats and 28 destroyers. Across its eastern exit, in position to cross the T of an enemy approaching from the west, he placed Seventh Fleet's six old, shore-bombardment battleships—all but one veterans of Pearl Harbor—in a line flanked by eight cruisers. The issue was never in doubt. Both Nishimura's battleships and three of his destroyers were blown out of the water. Shima's echelon, following 40 miles astern, prudently retired. By 0430 on 25 October, the southern arm of the Japanese pincers had been eliminated by the mighty U.S. force.

The elation felt in Seventh Fleet over this victory was extinguished a little more than two hours later, when the pagoda masts of Center Force's battleships appeared on the horizon north of Rear Admiral Clifton F. Sprague's Taffy 3, one of three groups of escort carriers operating off Samar. One of the epic actions in naval history was about to unfold. While Sprague's six little 18-knot carriers made away at flank speed, chasing rain squalls and the towering, color-coded splashes of Japanese shells, aircraft arose from all three Taffies to harass the oncoming enemy, and the three destroyers and four destroyer escorts constituting Sprague's screen advanced with utmost gallantry to engage Kurita's battleships and cruisers. The small boys' attack threw the Japanese formation into confusion and disabled at least one cruiser. The Taffies' aircraft also scored, forcing three cruisers to drop out of the battle. Ultimately, however, it was inevitable that Center Force's superior speed and bigger guns would tell. By 0910 the *Gambler Bay* (CVE-73) had become the second carrier in the war to succumb to gunfire, the destroyer *Hoel* (DD-533) had also been sunk, and the destroyer *Johnston* (DD-557) and destroyer escort *Samuel B. Roberts* (DE-413) were sinking.

Throughout these desperate hours, Kinkaid bombarded Halsey with calls for help. Informing him of events in Surigao Strait in a message sent at 0412, Kinkaid had sought confirmation that TF-34 was covering San Bernardino Strait. Halsey, who had given the order to form TF-34 during his run north, did not receive this communication until 0648. Perplexed by Kinkaid's query, Halsey replied that TF-34 was with his carriers, "now engaging enemy carriers," against which Mitscher had begun launching an hour earlier. By the time his answer reached Kinkaid, Center Force was engaging Taffy 3. Halsey learned of the action under way off Samar from a signal received from Kinkaid at 0822 and followed eight minutes later by an urgent request for the fast battleships. To a vexed Halsey it seemed that Kinkaid's 18 escort carriers and six old battleships should be able to cope with Center Force. Furthermore, whatever damage Center Force could do would have been done long before the fast battleships could reach the scene. Nevertheless, at 0848 he ordered TG-38.1, which had been trying to overtake the battle from an opening position 600 miles east of the Philippines, to make "best possible speed" to strike Center Force. Kinkaid was not assuaged, and at about 1000 his appeals climaxed in an anguished, plain-language WHERE IS LEE X SEND LEE.

Within minutes, Halsey received an even more electrifying signal. Sent by Admiral Nimitz, with information copies to Kinkaid and King, it read: WHERE IS RPT WHERE IS TASK FORCE THIRTY-FOUR RR THE WORLD WONDERS.

Halsey ordered all six fast battleships and TG-38.2 to turn south. At that moment, only 42 miles separated Northern Force from TF-34's big guns. Mitscher was left to press the action with two carrier groups and a surface action group of four cruisers and ten destroyers.

The terrible irony was that, although it would not be evident for hours, by then the crisis off Samar had passed. At 0911 Kurita broke off the pursuit of Taffy 3, convinced that it was one of Halsey's task groups. Apparently, he intended merely to reform his force, disordered by the Taffies' counterattacks, but at 0945 a false report from naval headquarters in Manila inspired him to go looking for another U.S. carrier group supposedly located not far to the north. The phantom force eluded him, and, after a series of fruitless countermarches during which three heavily damaged cruisers went down, Kurita decided to withdraw. At 2140, Center Force reentered San Bernardino Strait. The van of TF-34 reached there at 0100, in time to sink a laggard destroyer.

ADAPTED FROM "... 50 YEARS AGO: LEYTE GULF," U.S. NAVAL INSTITUTE *PROCEEDINGS*, OCTOBER 1994

their normal gasoline load.") Failures in water pressure and the automatic sprinkler system allowed the fire to rage uninterrupted. Heavy black smoke entered the forward engine room, filling the space "to the point of suffocation and darkness."

The *Princeton* was the first carrier to be hit while under Big Mamie's protection. As she burned, enemy air attacks continued. At 1017 bombs from a Judy near missed the *Langley*. Other strikes at 1300 and 1510 inflicted no additional damage. The *Princeton*, however, was a lost cause. Secondary explosions also damaged the *Birmingham* (CL-62) and *Morrison* (DD-560), which had come alongside to remove personnel.

To the north, the Battle of the Visayna Sea was under way, which resulted in the loss to the Japanese of the large battleship *Musashi*. As the *Massachusetts*'s war diary noted, the commanders of TF 38, particularly Halsey, placed too much reliance on the overly optimistic reports of their airmen: "Preliminary reports indicated that our planes had done extensive damage to units of the Jap force in waters east of Mindoro Island."

Thus, when scouts finally spotted Japanese carriers acting as a decoy force to the north, and believing that the surface threat had been dealt with, Halsey collected his full available strength, which included the *Iowa*, *New Jersey*, *Washington*, *Massachusetts*, *South Dakota*, and *Alabama*, along with six cruisers led by Rear Admiral Whiting in the *Vincennes* (CL-64) and Desrons 50 and 52, and on 25 October TG 34.1 steamed north together to chase down this perceived threat.

The plain prose of the battleship's war diary captures best what happened next.

"While reports from our planes indicated that severe damage had been inflicted upon the portion of the Japanese Fleet to the north of us, other reports from Commander Seventh Fleet revealed that a considerable force of enemy ships had passed through San Bernardino Straits during the night and was attacking Seventh Fleet Forces in waters east of Samar Island." This unexpected

Coming into Ulithi Anchorage on 24 November 1944, during a break in operations off the Philippines. Photographed from the USS *Wasp*; Fleet Admiral Chester W. Nimitz has autographed the original print (U.S. Navy)

Liberty on the beach at Ulithi. On this day, at least, swimming and sunbathing seem to be the only activities under way. (U.S. Navy Cruise Book)

attack finally caused Halsey to order TG 38.2 and the battleships to turn south. It was too late even though he pushed ahead with his two 33-knot battleships and left the *Massachusetts* and her four 27-knot sisters to follow.

The only surface action that the mighty surface forces of the Third Fleet saw came when Whiting's Crudiv 14 caught the Japanese destroyer *Nowaki*, which was straggling after rescuing survivors from the Battle off Samar. The *Vincennes*, followed by the *Biloxi* (CL-80) and *Miami* (CL-89), annihilated her in five minutes. Whiting erroneously reported that the enemy vessel was a heavy cruiser of the *Aoba* or *Atago* class.

On 27 October the fast battleships rendezvoused with nine tankers and their attendant escort carriers. After that, the *Massachusetts*, in company with TG 38.3, headed for Ulithi. The first phase of the Philippine campaign was over. It was not particularly successful for Big Mamie as she had missed the long anticipated surface action, and in her only serious air action, one of the carriers in her care had been sunk.

The *Massachusetts* anchored in Ulithi on 1 November, but she did not stay long, being called to support TG 38.1 as it hit targets on northern Luzon from the 4th through the 6th. This group consisted of the *Wasp* (CV-18), *Hornet*, *Cowpens*, *Monterey*, *Massachusetts*, *Alabama*, three cruisers, and Desrons 61 and 46. There was a submarine scare on the 5th. Also on that day a kamikaze crashed the *Lexington* of TG 38.3; she was still able to maintain her place in formation.

An approaching typhoon caused the task force to break off operations on the 8th and head north. On the 11th, however, TG 38.1 was back on the line, hitting Ormoc Bay through which the Japanese were reinforcing Leyte. The *Massachusetts* and her group kept a fueling rendezvous on the 12th, followed by two more days of air strikes in the central Philippines.

In the early morning of 19 November an Emily got near enough for the *Massachusetts* to engage the aircraft with her 5-inch battery. The plane veered away, and a night fighter finally splashed it. This was the last day in the task group's offensive against the central Philippines. On the way back to Ulithi, the *Massachusetts* and *Alabama* exercised their main batteries by taking turns firing on each other's wakes. The *Massachusetts* spent the rest of November at anchor.

On 1 December the *Massachusetts* got under way as part of Task Group 38.1: the *Yorktown* (flagship of Rear Admiral A. E. Montgomery), *Wasp*, *Langley*, *Cowpens*, *Massachusetts* (flagship of Rear Admiral G. B. Davis), *Alabama*, Crudiv 6 with four cruisers, and Desron 53, but she immediately lost a propeller shaft due to a hot spring bearing. Her men fixed this

Halsey's Typhoon

The sea was anything but pacific when I stepped on the *Nehenta Bay*'s (CVE-74) bridge to take over the watch again at 0800. Never before had I seen a day like that one. Mountains of angry water rushed against one another, surging and writhing together. Masses of water, unbelievable in size, hurled themselves at the ship, tossing it about like an autumn leaf in the wind. The water boiled, and from the top of every wave, the full gale, which was howling so that one had to shout to be heard, blew sheets of spray to mingle with the rain and thick mist that hung low on the water. Visibility had dropped to a few hundred yards.

Soon after this watch began it was apparent that we'd been overtaken by a typhoon—the most dreaded force in the Pacific. Already, all plans for completing the refueling had been abandoned, as had any thought of launching any aircraft, though we were close to some of Japan's most powerful airbases. Controlling the ships themselves had become the principal consideration on the bridges of all vessels in the area, of which there must have a hundred.

The barometer, 29.40 at 0900, was steadily dropping; every quarter-hour check showed it lower. The wind was now a steady 60 knots, with gusts up to 75. The waves, where they could be distinguished through the shroud of mist, were rising to 40 and 50 feet. As they took the ship from behind, running up under her, they lifted the screws clear of the water and flung the carrier head down into the churning trough.

Soon . . . we were alone. We could see nothing but the pall of the mist and the savage anger of the sea. The latter was now lashed into such a fury of foam that the blown spume across the ragged shapes of the waves looked like the streaked drifting of blizzard-driven snow. The barometer was down to 29.20 and still tumbling. (It would reach 29.12 before I left the bridge that day.) The wind was causing the arrow on the gauge to hit the top—80 knots—and quiver there, and its sound had become a penetrating shriek that rose by piercing octaves. A man could not stand against that wind. The crew on the flight deck, striving desperately to lash down those of our aircraft that we had not been able to take below, lay on the deck and clung to lines like men in the tide of a wave, and where the driven spray struck the face or other uncovered skin, it stung like needles.

The feeling on the bridge was tense as we stood peering ahead and seeing less than our own ship's length through the thick mist that swirled and eddied around us. Every man was walled off from the others about him by the roar of the tempest; each was thinking his own thoughts and seeing his fears reflected in the taut faces of the others.

One could see that the ship could not hold together if we continued much longer as we were going. She was shaking all over with each rush into the trough of the sea. Already, seams were opening. One in the side plating on the hangar deck had given way, fortunately well above the waterline. Another opened in the deck on the fantail, over which green sea water was pouring. The men in the steering engine room, just below the latter, were calling for a bucket brigade to help them bail.

The ship had to be brought into the wind and held there with only enough speed to maintain steering control. Word was passed to all hands by means of the public announcing system that we were to come about. No one had to be told what to expect when the ship came broadside to a sea like that.

The ship's skipper had taken the con, and he now gave the order to the helmsman. Slowly, the ship began to swing into the wind. Every man clung to his support until his knuckles were white. For several long minutes, the tension lasted while nothing particularly remarkable happened. Then, suddenly, as though the sea had only just observed that we had put ourselves in its grasp, an enormous wave coming up on the quarter picked up the ship as a puppy picks up an old shoe. Lifting us aloft so that the screws, free of the water, caused the ship to vibrate to its keel, the wave threw us crashing into the teeth of a crosswave toward our starboard bow. Down went the bow, engulfed in green seawater, as the ship shuddered and we held our breaths, clinging to our supports until our arms ached.

For agonizing seconds, the ship lay on her side. Twenty feet above the flight deck, those of us on the bridge, feeling the full effect of the roll, waited with something tight about our hearts, seriously wondering whether the ship would right itself. Finally, hesitantly at first and then more surely, the uproll began. Then came the list in the other direction, seldom so bad as that to starboard because of the weight of the carrier's island. Then down again to starboard, as another wall of water struck the bow and a shiver went through the ship, but she did not go down so far this time. Over again to port and back to starboard, shuddering and quaking so that her groans and the grinding of steel on steel could be heard even over the howl of the gale.

Slowly, however, the *Nehenta Bay* was coming about. The ship, nevertheless, was in irons, locked in the teeth of the typhoon. We had full control of engines and rudder, yet from that moment until the storm began to abate, she was out of our control.

Then, to turn terror into near-panic, reports began to come up from radar plot of ships about us. Suddenly there were vessels on all sides coming toward us. One went by to starboard only a half-mile away. That's too close for comfort with heavy ships in low visibility. Almost immediately another went by to port, even closer this time. Then there were ships ahead coming directly toward us. We lay there in irons, unable to maneuver, as radar plot reported minute by minute.

"Ship, dead ahead, 800 yards, closing."

It was now apparent that, in coming about into the wind, we had turned directly into the path of Task Force 38 steaming downwind before the storm. We were surrounded by ships in all directions.

"Ship, dead ahead, 600 yards, closing."

There, slightly off the port bow, a battleship loomed through the mist only a few hundred yards ahead.

ADAPTED FROM "BATTLING THE PACIFIC'S MOST DEADLY FORCE," *NAVAL HISTORY*, OCTOBER 2008

The bow of the *Massachusetts* pushing through green seas during a Pacific typhoon (U.S. Navy Cruise Book)

problem at sea, but the battleship returned to Ulithi on 2 December nonetheless. She did not return to action until 10 December. After several days of exercises, TG 38.1 approached Luzon on the 14th and launched a series of attacks that continued through the 17th. The Japanese did not retaliate to these strikes. On 18 December another typhoon struck the fleet, making it impossible to refuel. The *Massachusetts* diary gives only a dry taste of what it must have been like: "By 0800 visibility was limited to a few hundred yards and the storm had increased to such proportions that some of the ships began to report personnel lost over the side and the sustaining of material damage. At 0912 the *Monterey* reported all the planes on her hangar deck to be on fire and the loss of a gun director. Shortly thereafter she reported loss of steering control and that she was dead in the water." The *Cowpens* also suffered a fire on her hangar deck. She dropped out of formation. "At 1030 an unidentified ship was detected by radar drifting through the formation. Avoiding action was taken, and at 1035 a CVE, apparently dead in the water was sighted about 500 yards off the starboard bow. An unsuccessful effort was made to communicate with the ship, later identified as *Rudyard Bay* (CVE-81)."

Conditions improved that afternoon and on the 19th fueling commenced. However, the storm had overwhelmed the *Hull* (DD-350), *Spence* (DD-512), and *Monaghan* (DD-354). Four light carriers, one light cruiser, and ten destroyers suffered significant damage. As the cripples headed out for Ulithi the fleet turned toward Luzon for more strike operations, steaming back through the same storm-churned waters looking for survivors. However, as the *Massachusetts*'s diary commented, "apparently the course followed toward tomorrow's strike position is taking the Task Force closer to the typhoon and into heavy swells resulting from it." Shortly after midnight on the 21st Halsey canceled the strike, and the fleet sought safer waters to the south. That morning one of the *Massachusetts*'s destroyers picked up 13 survivors from the *Hull*, "all in good condition with the exception of one man who had been bitten by a shark." TG 38.1 met the tankers on the 22nd and conducted exercises on the 23rd and 24th as it continued south toward Ulithi. The *Massachusetts* docked on Christmas Eve and remained in port provisioning and repairing the dings and bangs incurred by continuous operations and violent weather.

She was under way again on the 31st, however, and almost immediately suffered a casualty when a leak in the main condenser caused the boilers to begin salting. The *Massachusetts* dropped out of formation to correct the defect, accompanied by the *Maddox* (DD-731) and *Taussig* (DD-746). She locked No. 3 shaft at 1844 and started repairs. Thus passed New Year's Eve on the battleship.

Murderers' Row: Third Fleet aircraft carriers at anchor in Ulithi Atoll, 8 December 1944, during a break from operations in the Philippines area. The carriers are (from front to back): the ***Wasp***, ***Yorktown***, ***Hornet***, ***Hancock*** (CV-19), and ***Ticonderoga*** (CV-14). The ***Wasp***, ***Yorktown***, and ***Ticonderoga*** are all painted in camouflage Measure 33, Design 10a. (U.S. Navy)

ASIA AND THE HOME ISLANDS:

January–August 1945

NEW YEAR'S DAY 1945 FOUND THE *MASSACHUSETTS* STEAMING FROM ULITHI toward Formosa with Task Group 38.1: the carriers *Yorktown* (flagship of Rear Admiral A. W. Radford), *Wasp*, *Cabot*, and *Cowpens*; Batdiv 8 with the *Massachusetts* (flagship of Rear Admiral J. F. Shafroth Jr.) and *South Dakota*; Crudivs 6 and 10; and two destroyer squadrons. After taking on 204,758 gallons of fuel on 2 January, the *Massachusetts* screened the carriers as they began launching fighters on the 3rd. Squally weather and a low ceiling, however, forced cancellation of bomber operations that day and the next. TF 38 then turned south to hammer airfields in Northern Luzon. These raids continued throughout the 6th and 7th as Formosa remained socked in. On the 8th the *Massachusetts* refueled. Standing by the carriers was thirsty work, although she was dispensing oil to destroyers nearly every day herself.

Japanese ships aflame near Kamranh Bay, French Indochina, 21 January 1945, after being attacked by planes of the USS *Wasp* (U.S. Navy)

The carriers finally were able to hit Formosa on 9 January. On the 11th TF 38 began a high-speed run south toward Kamranh Bay (Cam Ranh Bay) in French Indochina. Captain Warlick told the crew: "As you all know, we have now entered the South China Sea. This is a step of tremendous importance in advancing the war. It is of greater importance, for example, than the first raid on Truk and Saipan." He went on to explain how sea power was the control of maritime lines of communication and how by the fleet's advance, Japan's routes to the resource-rich areas of the south would be cut. "In a sense we may consider that the Navy's objective in crossing the Pacific Ocean has been to arrive at this goal. . . . Tomorrow morning we will be in a position to strike at the dense shipping which skirts the coast of Indochina, carrying the riches of the Indies to Japan. In the next few days we shall destroy the seaborne trade of Japan from Saigon to Hongkong."

The Americans hoped to confront the Japanese carrier-battleships *Ise* and *Hyuga*. The fast battleships gathered to take them on, but the Japanese had no interest in fighting the American battle line with a couple of hybrids, and a surface battle did not materialize. TF 38's bombers, however, caught three convoys at sea and sank nine escorts, seven tankers, and four cargo ships. They dispatched another nine vessels

A dramatic image of the *Massachusetts* pushing through heavy seas, taken from one of her escorting destroyers. A light carrier is visible beyond her. (U.S. Navy Cruise Book)

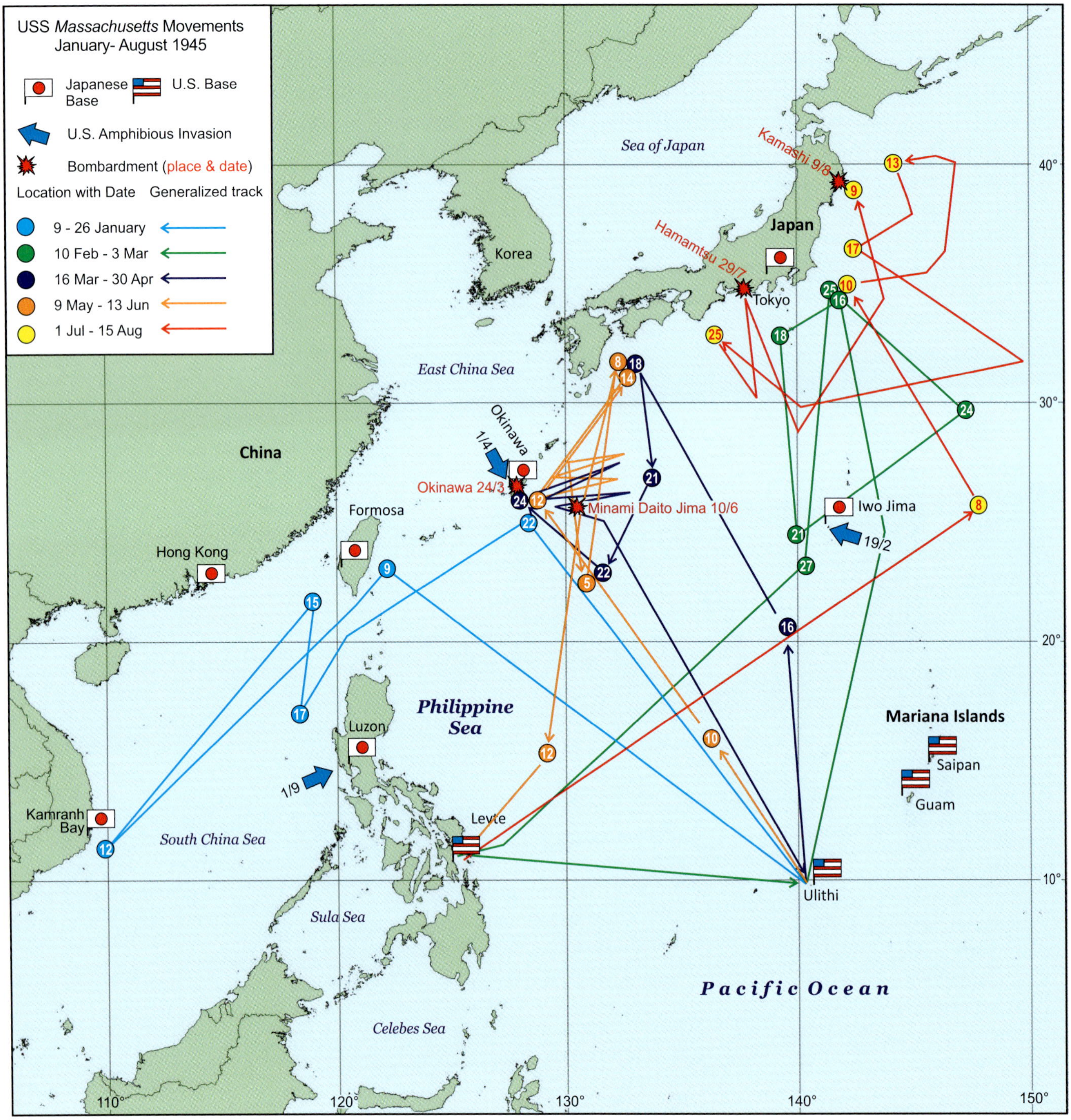

This chart shows the movements of the *Massachusetts* from 9 January 1945 when she departed Ulithi to support aerial strikes against Formosa to the end of the war. During these months she rampaged over a massive area extending 40° of longitude from west to east and 30° north to south supporting the strikes of the fast carries, conducting four bombardments and supporting three landings.

in port. The French light cruiser *Lamotte-Picquet* was swept up in the carnage and sent to the bottom as well. TF 38 then retired unscratched. As it withdrew north it struck Hong Kong, Amoy, and the Swatow area of southern China along the way on 15 and 16 January.

On 17 January the fleet experienced heavy swells off Luzon. Fueling operations had to be suspended, and the weather damaged several destroyers. After conditions improved the 3rd Fleet debouched into the Philippine Sea on the 20th. That day the Japanese made several air attacks, and for the first time in 1945 the *Massachusetts* fired her 5-inch, 40-mm, and 20-mm weapons on a single aircraft that had the temerity to approach her starboard bow. As the fleet launched strikes against Formosa on the 21st, the *Massachusetts* observed Japanese aircraft attacking other units, but no targets approached within range of her guns.

On 26 January the *Massachusetts* entered Ulithi and anchored. She took on supplies, repaired her main injection valve grid, and granted such liberty as the atoll's slender attractions could offer.

On 10 February the *Massachusetts* was under way as part of TG 58.1, heading north to support the landings on Iwo Jima. Once again Captain Warlick addressed his men. He explained that the Philippine campaign was over for the *Massachusetts* and that they were returning to the Central Pacific Campaign. "We are now en route to our usual task of paving the way. Where the landing will be will become clear in a few days."

On 16 February TG 58 began launching fighters for a predawn sweep over airfields in the Tokyo-Yokohama area. This was the first U.S. carrier air strike on Japan's capital since the Doolittle Raid in April 1942. Dive and torpedo bombers followed. At 0710 the *Massachusetts* detected an enemy picket boat 15,000 yards away. This proved to be *Patrol Craft 36*, which the destroyer *Haynesworth* (DD-700) dispatched expending 292 rounds in the process. The *Haynesworth* then took care of the picket boat *Wafu Maru* and rescued 11 survivors. No enemy aircraft approached within 25,000 yards of the battleship. The Americans repeated their strikes the next day and then set course for Iwo Jima to help soften up that island. Those strikes occurred over 20 and 21 February. Japanese aircraft attacked elements of TF 58 but kept clear of the *Massachusetts*.

On 23 February the *Massachusetts* bunkered 279,755 gallons of fuel oil and then, following exercises, she turned north for another go at Tokyo. The carriers launched strikes on the 25th, but heavy snow in the target area minimized their effectiveness. The task group headed toward Kobe, but the weather was bad there as well. The ships retired south having accomplished little in their second attack against the Japanese Home Islands.

The first of March saw TG 58.1, now consisting of the *Hornet*, *Wasp*, *Bennington* (CV-20), and *Belleau Wood* with Batdiv 8, the *Massachusetts* and *Indiana*; the cruisers *Vincennes*, *Miami*, and *San Juan*; and Desrons

Few images capture the might and power of the late-war U.S. Navy better than this one of the fleet at anchor in Ulithi (U.S. Naval Institute Photo Archive)

Boxing match held while under way. Boxing was probably the most popular spectator sport in the fleet. (U.S. Navy Cruise Book)

A carrier pilot successfully plucked from the sea by a *Massachusetts* SOC. (U.S. Navy Cruise Book)

The USS *Haynesworth* (DD-700), a *Sumner*–class destroyer, joined the 3rd/5th Fleet at Ulithi in December 1944 and was one of the *Massachusetts*'s regular escorts for the next three months. (U.S. Navy)

The *Massachusetts* under way with Task Force 58.1 on 12 February 1945, en route to raid Tokyo. Ships of Task Group 58.3 are in the background. (U.S. Navy)

A 5-inch mount with ejected shell casings littering the deck around it. Firing in full automatic a 2-gun mount could generate 40 such casings in just a minute. (U.S. Navy Cruise Book)

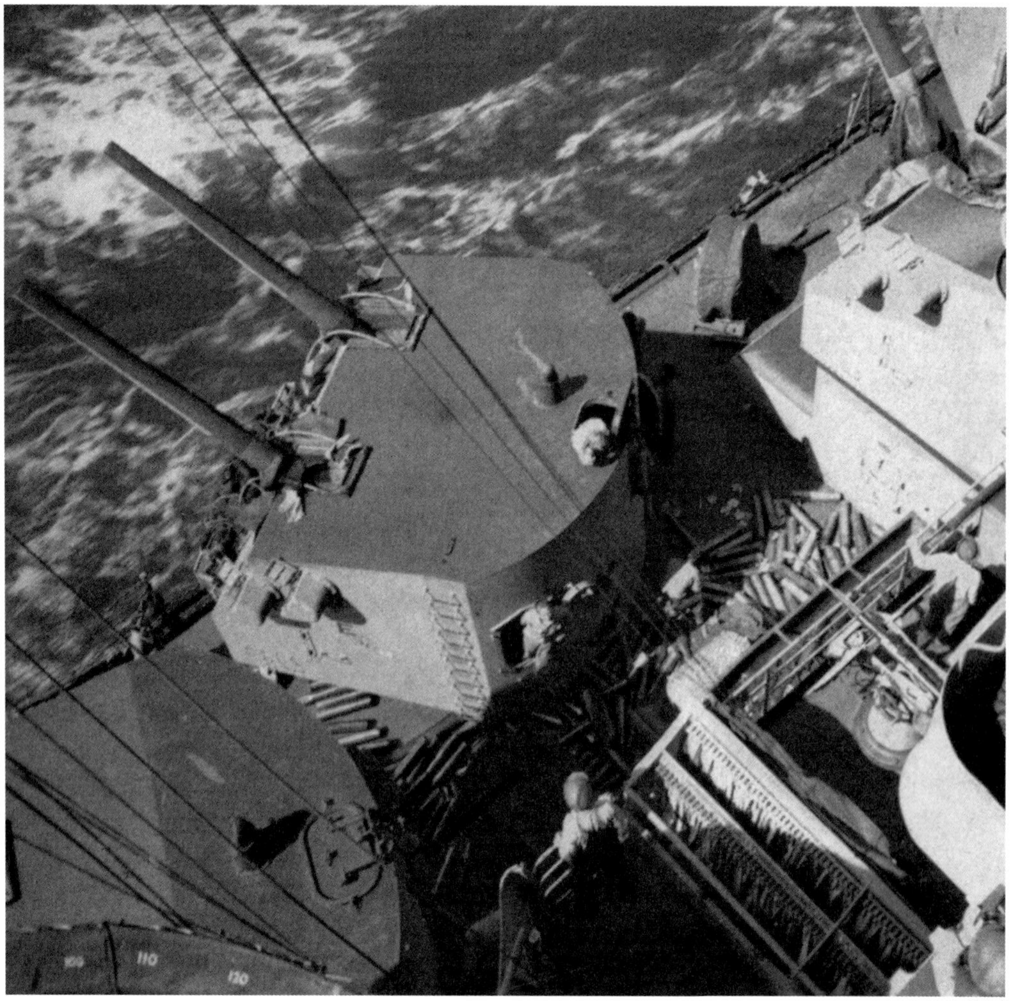

61 and 25 launching air strikes on Okinawa—the relentless American offensive's next target. On the 1st a *Massachusetts* Kingfisher rescued a *Bennington* pilot who had splashed southwest of Okinawa.

On the 3rd, during the return to Ulithi, the battle line formed to practice surface warfare evolutions. The mighty force included eight fast battleships, eight cruisers, and nine destroyer divisions. The big ships improved their gunnery skills as the destroyers simulated torpedo attacks. On 16 March, after a quick turnaround in Ulithi, the *Massachusetts* was again a member of TG 58.1, with much the same organization as during the strikes off Tokyo. Just before dawn on 18 March, when TG 58.1 was 240 miles east of Kyushu, Japanese aircraft attacked. This was the largest air raid the *Massachusetts* had experienced in months. One plane buzzed the battleship, and Big Mamie damaged another that crossed her stern heading for the *Wasp*. This Nell crashed just 50 yards short of the big carrier. At 0725 the *Massachusetts* shot down another dive bomber that was after the *Hornet*. During that day the carriers struck Japanese facilities on Kyushu. At 1311 the *Massachusetts* shot down another aircraft attacking the *Hornet*. Her Kingfishers also plunked a downed USS *Franklin* (CV-13) pilot from the drink. In her final action, the *Massachusetts* fired on a group of bogies at 2226 and saw one aircraft burst into flames and crash 8,000 yards off her port quarter.

The next day, 19 March, was just as frantic. The battleship engaged enemy night bombers at 0418. At 0708 "an enemy plane dove out of the clouds and dropped a bomb which hit the *Wasp*. . . . This ship took the enemy plane, a Judy, under fire but was not able to destroy it." The bomb penetrated the flight deck amidships and the hangar deck and exploded after passing through the second deck, blowing a 16-by-24-foot hole in the second deck and a 19-by-22-foot hole in the third deck. Two aircraft were destroyed and 30 damaged, and 102 men died, but the carrier was back in action within an hour. However, on this strike TF 58

Taken from the USS *Wasp*, a Japanese aircraft literally dropping from the sky. The flash of antiaircraft fire can be seen from the battleship on the lower right-hand corner of the photograph. (U.S. Navy Fold 3); (inset) The USS *Wasp* at the moment she was hit by a Japanese bomber. (U.S. Navy Fold 3)

Okinawa

The World War II battle for Okinawa is unique in the annals of warfare. For it was there in the spring of 1945 that one nation attempted to annihilate the sea and air forces of her enemies by the almost exclusive use of suicide attacks. For 82 days the battle raged. For 82 days the finest young men of Japan flew off to certain death in the skies and waters about Okinawa. And for 82 days the officers and men of the U. S. Navy fought savagely and brilliantly to fend them off. It is a fact that the kamikazes left their mark; it is also a fact that they could not dislodge the "fleet that came to stay."

Okinawa is the largest, most populous island in the Nansei Shoto (Ryukyu) chain. Situated only 350 miles from industrial Kyushu, 845 miles from Tokyo, and 1,210 miles from U.S. B-29 bases on Saipan, it offered numerous sites for airfields from which almost any type of plane could operate. It also provided several excellent naval anchorages, and its possession by the Allies would lead to the severance of Japanese communications with Formosa, Korea, and the Chinese mainland. But Okinawa's greatest importance stemmed from the fact, well understood by the Japanese, that it would provide the necessary staging area for the planned invasion of Japan.

The desperate situation which would threaten the Japanese if the U.S. assault on Okinawa were successful stimulated them to their greatest and most fanatical effort. One hundred twenty thousand men stood ready to defend the island, with every possible plane, and the remnants of the Imperial Fleet. Allied forces, under the command of Admiral Raymond A. Spruance, USN, consisted of 548,000 men of the Army, Navy, and Marine Corps, 339 combatant ships (including 21 units of the British Pacific Fleet), and 1,139 auxiliary vessels. Of the Okinawa operation Fleet Admiral E. J. King wrote, "from any standpoint [it] was the most difficult ever undertaken by our forces in the Pacific." The Japanese were convinced that suicide attacks were the only means at their command which might prove effective against U.S. ships. But in order to understand the reasons behind this belief, it is necessary to go back six months to October 1944, and the Battle for Leyte Gulf. At that time the odds were tremendously against Japan. Her early supremacy, based on control of the sea, had long since waned. In June 1944, in the Battle of the Philippine Sea, the Japanese fleet had suffered an overwhelming defeat. Japan's only offensive resources were her land-based air fleets, whose pilots were pitifully inexperienced, and the fire power of her surface ships, which lacked the support of carrier planes. Everyone was aware that it would take a miracle to save the empire from disaster. It was becoming apparent that neither surface, carrier, bomber, nor submarine forces could perform that miracle.

An entry dated 18 October 1944, in the personal diary of Admiral Kimpei Teraoka (at that time Commander, First Air Fleet) summed up the Japanese feeling.

"We can no longer (resist) by adhering to conventional methods of warfare. . . . Instead, we must steel ourselves against weakness. . . . If fighter pilots set an example by volunteering for special attack missions, other units will follow suit. These examples will, in turn, inspire surface and army forces. . . . We conclude that the enemy can be stopped and our country saved only by crash-dive attacks on their ships."

On 25 October the Japanese were able to compare the relative effectiveness of conventional and suicide attacks; for on that day 93 fighters and 57 bombers inflicted no damage, while six kamikazes scored hits on three escort carriers. During the first three months of their operation, the kamikazes scored 121 hits and 53 damaging near-misses. The superiority of special attacks was manifest, and the Japanese belief was proven true. These early reports of kamikaze success caught the fancy of military leaders and the public—and the craze was on.

The USS *Bunker Hill* on fire after being crashed by a kamikaze aircraft off Okinawa on 11 May 1945. The USS *The Sullivans* (DD-537) is in the foreground. She closed the carrier and rescued 166 men forced over the side by the fire. (U.S. Naval Institute Photo Archive)

The first major action of the Okinawa campaign occurred between 18–21 March 1945, when the 82 ships of Task Force 58 carried out air strikes against Kyushu airfields and fleet units at Kure and Kobe. Five hundred twenty-eight enemy planes were destroyed; 16 enemy surface craft were damaged; and scores of hangars, factories, and warehouses were destroyed or damaged at a total cost of 116 American planes. This attack resulted in the Japanese being unable to mount any strong air attack against our forces for almost a week after the initial landings on Okinawa.

On 1April the assault troops landed over the Hagushi beaches and drove toward Yontan and Kadena airfields. On 6 and 7 April the divine wind struck with all the fury of an empire on the brink of disaster. In this first of nine general kamikaze attacks, 355 special attack planes, accompanied by almost as many conventional fighters and reconnaissance planes, bore down on Okinawa. In the two days of vicious battle, 22 kamikazes succeeded in crashing ships. Total Japanese losses are unknown, but it is estimated that nearly 300 were stopped at the picket line; and of this number it is estimated that 275 fell victim to Navy carrier pilots. But U.S. forces were not unscathed. Two destroyers, one high-speed minesweeper, and one LST went to the bottom; while 11 destroyers, one high-speed minesweeper, three escort vessels, three minesweepers, and the aircraft carrier *Hancock* were damaged.

During the next two months the U. S. Navy absorbed a pounding unlike any it had ever experienced. The divine wind struck no fewer than eight more times in general attacks; but after each onslaught the Navy buried its dead, cared for its wounded, replaced its sunken and battered ships, and rose to fight again.

By 10 June the battle was all but over, and the fast carriers set their course for Leyte Gulf. On June 21, 1945, 82 days after the initial landings, organized resistance came to an end, and the Island was declared secured.

EXTRACTED FROM "DIVINE WIND OVER OKINAWA," U.S. NAVAL INSTITUTE *PROCEEDINGS*, JUNE 1957

A formation of Curtiss SB2C Helldivers flying in formation. By 1944 they had replaced the SBD Dauntless in front-line units. (U.S. Navy Cruise Book)

suffered more damage than in any other attack during the war to date, inasmuch as the *Enterprise* and *Yorktown* also were hit by bombs and a kamikaze crashed the *Intrepid*. The *Franklin*, however, was roughed up worst of all. Two bombs struck her, and explosions ignited huge fires. Only heroic damage control saved the ship. The *Santa Fe* (CL-60) and *Hickox* (DD-673) suffered damage when they were alongside helping to fight the fires. The *Pittsburgh* (CA-72) towed her south at 6 knots, and the fleet stayed in company despite the danger to all. But the Japanese were only able to mount one more small attack several hours after dark. A large group of Bettys tried to attack on the 21st; American fighters intercepted and claimed the destruction of 26 bombers and 11 fighters. No enemy aircraft got within 10,000 yards of an American ship. The *Massachusetts*, however, did suffer a freak accident. At 2010, while making a sharp turn, a large wave broke over the stern and knocked the Kingfisher on the port catapult onto the deck, damaging it beyond repair.

While the crippled and damaged ships withdrew to Ulithi, TF 58 reorganized into three groups. FG 58.1 lost the *Wasp* but gained the *San Jacinto* (CVL-30), and on 23 March the fleet was back in action attacking Okinawa. The next day eight fast battleships bombarded shore installations. The *Massachusetts* opened fire at 0943 but left the line after three hours to recover her spotter aircraft. When the plane touched water a float collapsed and the aircraft nosed over. A destroyer rescued the pilot and radioman.

Following the bombardment, the crew was anxious to see the object of the ship's anger. One crewman recalled, "Nothing was firing back at us. We were experiencing no difficulties. We were practically dead in the water. We had been pounding them for some time with our 16-inch guns and we secured from general quarters. Well, everybody wanted to go and see the island. See what we'd been doing. So everybody rushed topside and were on the starboard side looking out over the island and the ship started to roll a bit and all of a sudden the 16-inch guns which had been heading out toward the island were heading closer and closer to the water. And they had to call general quarters again to right the ship. Two thousand men on one side, plus the guns, of course, were out that way too. That struck me as pretty funny."

Operations off Okinawa continued until the 28th when TF 58 took another swing north to hit Kyushu on the 29th. This time the fast carriers did not linger, beginning their retirement south at noon that day. Air strikes against Okinawa resumed on the 31st.

The landings on Okinawa occurred on 1 April. The *Massachusetts* was still part of TG 58.1, which consisted of the *Hornet*, *Bennington*, *Belleau Wood*, *San Jacinto*, Batdiv 8, Crudivs 10 and 14, and Desrons 61 and 25. Air operations continued through the 6th, with the *Massachusetts* firing one time on the 2nd at an enemy aircraft that buzzed the fleet before dawn. On the 6th a kamikaze missed the *Bennington*. The *Massachusetts* shot down a Zeke trying to attack the *Vincennes* and later another attacking the *San Jacinto*. No ships in TG 58.1 were damaged that day. On the 7th TG 58 spent its full strength attacking the *Yamato*, which had sortied from the north. The giant battleship absorbed terrific punishment but finally succumbed to at least 6 bombs and 11 torpedoes delivered by 380 carrier-borne aircraft.

On 8 April, in a demonstration of the ever-improving efficiency and scope of the U.S. Navy's underway replenishment capabilities, the *Massachusetts* took on 14 16-inch projectiles, 440 5-inch projectiles, and 464,795 gallons of fuel oil while under way. The next day she returned to the operational area, defending the carriers.

On 12 April TG 58.1 shot down two Zekes that tried to crash the *Indiana*. On the 13th a *Massachusetts* Kingfisher rescued another pilot. Despite a warning to expect heavy air attacks, none developed. On the 14th, however, Japanese aircraft broke through the fighter cover and one Zeke was shot down near the *Indiana* and another astern of the *Bennington*. No ships were damaged. There was another heavy air attack on the 16th. Lookouts on the battleship could observe fighters engaging Japanese aircraft 12 to 15 miles from the formation. Then several broke through. At 1201 an aircraft dove on the *San Jacinto* but broke off after the *Massachusetts*'s guns filled the skies around it with steel. Another Zeke drove on the *Massachusetts* at 1400 but was destroyed by fighters. It fell into the water 6,000 yards away.

On the 17th the *Massachusetts* took on 3,232 40-mm rounds, 58 16-inch rounds, and 532 5-inch rounds, along with 926,252 gallons of fuel oil. She continued to support operations ashore as part of TG 58.1, refueling destroyers every day and taking on more fuel and ammunition herself on the 22nd. There was a submarine scare on the 25th, an event that had become rare. She received more fuel and ammunition on the 27th. Finally, on 28 April, after nearly six weeks of sustained operations, the *Massachusetts* turned south for Ulthi, anchoring there on 30 April.

On 2 May there was another change of command ceremony as Captain John R. Redman relieved Captain Warlick. Redman had served as the communications officer on the staff of Admiral Chester Nimitz. The stopover in Ulthi was relatively brief. On 9 May the

On 2 May 1945, the last wartime captain of the *Massachusetts*, John R. Redman, replaces Captain Warlick. Redman had been the communications officer on the staff of Admiral Chester Nimitz. Rear Admiral J. F. Shafroth is on the left. (U.S. Navy Cruise Book)

Massachusetts was under way as flagship of Rear Admiral Shafroth and Task Unit 58.1.5, with the *Indiana*, *Alabama*, six cruisers, and three destroyer divisions. On 12 May Captain Redman addressed his crew. He told them the war was progressing well, but new challenges awaited as TF 58 headed north to seek strategic targets on Japanese soil. He also warned of new threats, such as the Baka bomb, a manned bomb dropped from a Betty and guided to its target by a suicide pilot.

On the next day, TF 58.1, which the *Massachusetts* had rejoined, was launching attacks on airfields in Kyushu. These had proved to be dangerous waters. On the 14th the battleship's antiaircraft batteries helped down three attackers that had penetrated the screen, including one that had targeted the battleship. On the 16th the *Massachusetts*'s Kingfisher rescued a downed carrier pilot. By the 17th TG 58.1 was off Okinawa again, supporting operations there. By this time the battleship's Kingfishers were accompanying fighter strikes so as to be at hand should rescues be required. This activity continued through 26 May with periodic refueling breaks. During this time Japanese air strikes failed to damage any ships in TG 58.1; in fact, attacks were fairly rare, with the *Massachusetts* only using her guns on the 25th.

On 28 May Vice Admiral Spruance hauled down his flag and Admiral Halsey took command, TF 58 becoming TF 38. The *Massachusetts* continued with TG 38.1, essentially the same formation as on 1 April. TG 38.1 continued to operate off Okinawa through the first days of June. The routine was interrupted on 4 June when, in the midst of refueling, orders came to retire southeast by south to avoid a typhoon reported to be southwest of the force. As the battleship's diary

A Japanese Betty twin-engine bomber rigged to carry a Baka manned rocket-propelled bomb. This weapon was first used off Okinawa but as fearsome as the weapon seemed, it accounted for relatively few U.S. ships. In its first operational use on 21 March 1945, the 16 carrier Bettys were all shot down before they could release their Bakas within the required 25 miles of a target. (U.S. Naval Institute Photo Archive)

tersely noted, "By 0100, 5 June 1945, the barometer had dropped to 29.42, the wind was force 7, causing a heavy swell. . . . At about 0630 the wind increased to an estimated 100 knots. A number of ships reported having serious difficulty, *Pittsburgh*, losing her bow and *Duluth* (CL-87) having her bow buckled." The *Massachusetts* passed through the eye of the storm at 0700. Although the wind dropped and the visibility rose, "seas in the typhoon's eye were mountainous, being much greater even than those encountered when the wind was estimated at 100 knots." However, despite the damage to the fleet, which included the loss of several destroyers, the *Massachusetts*'s principal casualty was only the loss of one Kingfisher.

Despite a general battering, the fleet continued to operate, and on 8 June TF 38's fighters swept over Kyushu. On the 10th Batdiv 8—the *Massachusetts*, *Indiana*, and *Alabama*—and Desdiv 121 bombarded Minami Daito Jima. The main battery fired 15 salvos, expending 81 16-inch shells, from 0620 to 0724. This damaged or destroyed several buildings. The secondary battery fired from 0728 to 0800, expending 100 rounds in 20 salvos, targeting a radio tower, an ammunition dump, and the town. Afterward the *Massachusetts* started south, and on 13 June she anchored in San Pedro Bay, Leyte Gulf. Here on the 19th Rear Admiral Shafroth transferred his flag to the *South Dakota*.

On 1 July the *Massachusetts* raised anchor and headed north in company with the *South Dakota* and *Indiana*, five cruisers, and ten destroyers. She joined with TF 38 the next day and on 3 July once again became part of TG 38.1 with the *Bennington*, *Lexington*, *Hancock*, *Belleau Wood*, and *San Jacinto*. In addition to the three battleships there were seven cruisers and Desrons 61 and 25. On 9 July Captain Redmon addressed his crew. He said that the Okinawa operation was concluded and no longer required TF 38's support. However, "continuous pressure must be exerted against the enemy. . . . Task Force 38 is stronger than ever this time. We have three groups each containing five carriers. We have a total of eight fast battleships, many new cruisers, and a much more comfortable number of destroyers than last time. Tomorrow morning at dawn from waters east of Tokyo we will send many air strikes against that area. . . . There may be a violent reaction to our visit. It is our job to take care of any that get by the aircraft patrols." He then informed the crew that they would be heading north after that to bombard Hokkaido and, finally, although "there has been nothing official, I feel certain . . . we will be the next fast battleship to go back [to the States for maintenance]."

The air strikes against targets in the Tokyo area commenced on 10 July. Despite expectations, the *Massachusetts* did not face any retaliatory raids. On 14 July the *South Dakota*, *Indiana*, and *Massachusetts*, two heavy cruisers, and four destroyers separated to bombard iron works at Kamaishi on the island of Honshu, north of Tokyo. Land was in view by 0842. The *Massachusetts*

Shelling Japan

There were no planes, no ships and only a timid spattering of fire from shore batteries to oppose them. The big battlewagons, their 16-inch guns pumping ton after ton of high explosive shells into targets that flamed erupted and collapsed, paraded brazenly only a few hundred yards off shore, completely ignoring the fact that the shore was the enemy's Japan.

For two ear-splitting hours, beginning at noon on 14 July, the 35,000-ton battleships *Massachusetts*, *Indiana*, and *South Dakota*, the cruisers *Chicago* and *Quincy*, and the destroyers *Black*, *Erben*, *Heermunn*, and *Southerland* pounded away at Kamaishi, vital steel port on the island of Honshu 275 miles north of Tokyo

Targets, for the 16-, 8- and 5-inch rifles of the fleet were the huge Kamaishi steel mill and dockyards sprawling along the water's edge. When the ships finally put back to sea, after steaming in sight of the coast for more than five hours, the steel mill was completely demolished and adjacent coke ovens were blazing furiously.

The assault was the first surface attack on Japan since 1863, when three American warships destroyed a shore battery that had been firing on neutral shipping.

Just as had carrier-borne aircraft in previous attacks, the fleet caught the enemy completely by surprise. Following a heavy carrier raid on Tokyo four days before, Tokyo radio confidently gushed that the 3rd Fleet was heading south, only to have it turn up in the north with more bombs dropped in coordination with the fleet shelling.

ADAPTED FROM *ALL HANDS*, AUGUST 1945

A Kingfisher being hoisted aboard the *Massachusetts*. (U.S. Navy Cruise Book)

A salvo of six 16-inch shells fired against the iron-works at Kamaishi, Japan. (U.S. Navy Cruise Book)

opened fire at 1213, and through 1409 she expended 300 HC 16-inch rounds. On the 15th the air targets were located in northern Honshu and Hokkaido. Once again, the battleships cruised unmolested off the Japanese coast. On the 17th, after refueling, the fast carriers launched waves of bombers and fighters that blanketed Japanese air installations in the Tokyo area. The strikes continued on the 18th. The worse threat the *Massachusetts* faced this entire time was a drifting mine that passed close aboard to starboard. One sailor remembered, "There was a Marine stationed on the bow. He had earphones. He'd spot the mines and he shot 'em with his rifle, but you had to hit 'em right on the little peddle. So, we're heading right for this mine, the battleship, and he was shooting but couldn't hit it so we did an emergency turn, the right side full speed ahead and the left side reverse and we just turned on a dime and the ship lay over and as it lay over the [wash] hit the mine and the shrapnel just sprayed on the deck. We had a few injuries on that one. That was pretty spooky."

After retiring several hundred miles to refuel "re-ammunition," and perform some maintenance (the *Massachusetts* fixed a condenser leak), the fleet steamed toward southern Honshu to hit the Japanese fleet units in the inland sea. These strikes commenced on 25 July and were repeated on the 28th. On the 29th the fleet once again targeted Tokyo. The only ammunition the *Massachusetts* expended was in drills and practice shoots.

The big guns went into action on 29 July when, in company of the *South Dakota* and *Indiana* and with four heavy cruisers and destroyers, the *Massachusetts* headed for Hamamatsu, south of Tokyo, her target being the Japanese Musical Instrument Company. She opened fire with her main battery at 2319 on the 29th and continued firing until 0028 on the 30th, expending 270 rounds. The ship experienced no casualties to materiel or personnel; however, Big Mamie narrowly avoided a collision with the *Lexington* that evening. She refueled the next day and on 3 August, TF 38, which had been cruising south of Honshu, met with a logistic group. There was little action for the fleet in the early part of August, as fog and rain twice caused operations to be canceled. The crew anticipated orders to head east toward the United States at any time. There was a back-and-forth as ships transferred personnel to her for

The battleships contributed Marines and sailors for the first landing forces sent to the Japanese mainland following the Japanese surrender. (U.S. Navy Cruise Book)

The crew of the *Massachusetts* inspecting the Japanese battleship *Nagato* in Tokyo Bay. (U.S. Navy Cruise Book)

transportation home and took equipment and supplies as the ship was cannibalized. But Big Mamie's war was not over yet.

On 9 August she participated in another bombardment of Kamashi, opening fire at 1254 and expending 265 HC 16-inch rounds through 1445. There were no casualties. At 1603 her antiaircraft battery went into action against a Judy, the first aircraft the ship had engaged in months.

There were air strikes against targets in northern Honshu and on Hokkaido on the 10th. Despite rumors of an imminent Japanese surrender, more raids on the Tokyo area followed on the 13th. The carriers launched strikes on the 15th, when word arrived from Third Fleet command that offensive operations against the Japanese had ceased and all strikes were recalled.

On the 16th "the three Task Groups of Task Force 38 and the British Task Group closed distance and were maneuvered simultaneously by signal direct from ComTask Force 38 in order that pictures might be taken from aircraft from 1100 to 1200." TF 38 remained off the coast of Japan; the carriers continued to fly combat air patrols and the battleships performed gunnery exercises. On the 19th the *Massachusetts* sent her Marine detachment of 95 men for temporary duty with the American forces making the initial landings on Japan. One officer recalled, "every ship provided a small contingent to go ashore and secure the Japanese home islands. It was a little strange, to put it mildly. All we had were some old Springfield rifles. We did have a Marine contingent, and they went ashore. They must have looked pretty good, but our bluejackets, they didn't know anything about marching, they didn't know anything about handling a rifle, and the Japanese must have thought why did they quit when they did when they saw this motley crew coming ashore."

On the 23rd Captain Redman disappointed his crew, telling them their return to the States for overhaul had been postponed. "We can only do the job we have and see what happens." Over the next week the *Massachusetts* supported the carriers operating off North Honshu. Finally, on 28 August word arrived that the *Massachusetts* would be going home. It had been a long war. She had been there when the very first U.S. troops engaged in combat on foreign soil in the Old World, and some of her crew were the very first to land in Japan at the very end.

The diary entry for 3 September 1945 reads: "At 0800 set course of 045°(T), speed 16 knots and departed from area enroute Puget Sound via great circle." Ten days later, she dropped anchor in Washington.

WRAP-UP

THE *MASSACHUSETTS* SAILED FOR PUGET SOUND ON 3 September 1945, where she received her second overhaul and refit. The sense of urgency that had marked her first refit, 15 months earlier, was gone, and not until 28 January 1946 did she sail for California and then for Hampton Roads, arriving there on 22 April 1946.

Once in Virginia the ship began the protective mothballing process, which involved dehumidifying the machinery spaces and placing metal cocoons over the gun emplacements. The *Massachusetts* decommissioned on 27 March 1947, after slightly less than five years of service, and became a member of the Atlantic Reserve Fleet at Norfolk. During this period the Navy considered various plans to refurbish the battleship, including one to raise her speed to 33 knots by removing the after turret and expanding her machinery spaces. All such

The *Massachusetts* under way at six knots in Puget Sound, Washington, after her final overhaul, 22 January 1946. (U.S. Navy)

The *Massachusetts* laid up at the Norfolk Naval Shipyard, Virginia, on 3 January 1963. At that time she had been stricken from the Naval Vessel Register, but was awaiting preservation as a memorial. The USS *Uvalde* (APA-88) is at right. (U.S. Navy)

ideas, however, proved prohibitively expensive, and nothing came of them.

On 1 June 1962, the Navy announced plans to scrap the *Massachusetts*. This news galvanized a group led by an association of former crew members to try to save the ship. Their original intention was to dock her alongside the frigate USS *Constitution* in Boston, but no site there would accept her; in fact, it seemed that no one wanted the ship at all. Finally, the crew's association approached the mayor of Fall River, Massachusetts, and sold him on the idea of hosting what hopefully would turn out to be a major tourist attraction in the city, which had in the past decades seen its tax base eroded by a loss of industry. Once the site had finally been determined, there remained the problem of moving the ship there. Over a two-year period, the *Massachusetts* Memorial Committee raised $100,000 to pay for the cost of insuring and towing the battleship from Virginia to Fall River, with over half the contributions coming from Massachusetts schoolchildren. On 14 August 1965, the *Massachusetts* was towed to Fall River, where she became a memorial for the state's World War II dead. The crew's association began the long task of refurbishing the ship, which had suffered from a lack of maintenance, and restoring her, at least in appearance, to her World War II condition.

Since 1965 the *Massachusetts* has been the center of Battleship Cove: America's Fleet Museum and Maritime Museum, one of the most successful warship and maritime museums in the world. Battleship Cove's collection of ships has grown and today includes the destroyer USS *Joseph P. Kennedy Jr.* (DD-850), the submarine USS *Lionfish* (SS-298), the Soviet missile corvette *Hiddensee*, and PT boats *617* and *796*. More than 80,000 people visit the *Massachusetts* each year to view her unique and immersive compartments and exhibits. She actively preserves the memory of her service in the words of many of the men who served on board her and the memory of a period in American history where the deeds and accomplishments of the nation were truly epic. Even nearly 80 years after her keel was laid, she remains a marvel of engineering and technology.

FROM BATTLESHIP COVE

Following Operation Torch, *Massachusetts* transferred to the Pacific and spent the remainder of the war there, save for a brief overhaul at Bremerton in the middle of 1944. She decommissioned in March 1947 and rested for 18 years in the Portsmouth VA reserve fleet. Thanks to the intervention of former crew members, legislators, private citizens, and schoolchildren, she escaped several appointments with the scrapyard in the early 1960s and began her new life in Fall River, MA, on August 15, 1965, as our state's official World War II memorial.

Fast-forwarding to the present, *Massachusetts* is queen of the fleet at what is now known as Battleship Cove. Over the more than half century since her arrival, she's been joined by submarine *Lionfish*, destroyer *Joseph P. Kennedy, Jr.*, Russian-built corvette *Hiddensee*, PT Boats *617* and *796*, *LCM 56*, and two helicopters.

The challenges inherent in maintaining the latter are many in what is essentially a 24/7 operation. Beyond managing expected physical plant issues, staff and volunteers work continuously to create and maintain safe and sensible wayfinding and engaging interpretation for our visitors, preserve our huge collection of artifacts and documents, and most importantly, *keep the rust at bay*.

As for all of our peers in the museum-ship business, creative programming is key to sustainability. Our ships offer remarkable educational opportunities related to science, technology, history, and the humanities, and we strive to integrate these into our interpretations and public interactions. Related activities include behind-the-scenes tours, living history (re-enactor) weekends, and public and private school collaborations. Most significantly, our overnight camping program that debuted in 1972 remains relevant today as grandchildren and great-grandchildren seek knowledge about their forebears.

Ultimately, our vessels are memorials to those who served on and in them. As we move further away in time from those generations, we are focused more than ever on our primary mission to safeguard their memories. We consider it a privilege.

Christopher J Nardi
Chief Operating Officer
USS *Massachusetts* Memorial Committee Inc.

Damage from 8-inch projectile to inboard bulkhead of living space A-208L. (Christopher J. Nardi / USS *Massachusetts* Memorial Committee Inc.)

Looking up at patch in main deck where 8-inch shell penetrated from within an outboard bunkroom on the port side of A-208L. (Christopher J. Nardi / USS *Massachusetts* Memorial Committee Inc.)

Damage to bunk stanchion in outboard bunkroom on port side of A-208L. (Christopher J. Nardi / USS *Massachusetts* Memorial Committee Inc.)

Exhibited section of main deck where 8-inch shell penetrated and exploded within an outboard bunkroom on the port side of A-208L. (Christopher J. Nardi / USS *Massachusetts* Memorial Committee Inc.)

Damage to forward athwartships bulkhead in outboard bunkroom on port side of A-208L. (Christopher J. Nardi / USS *Massachusetts* Memorial Committee Inc.)

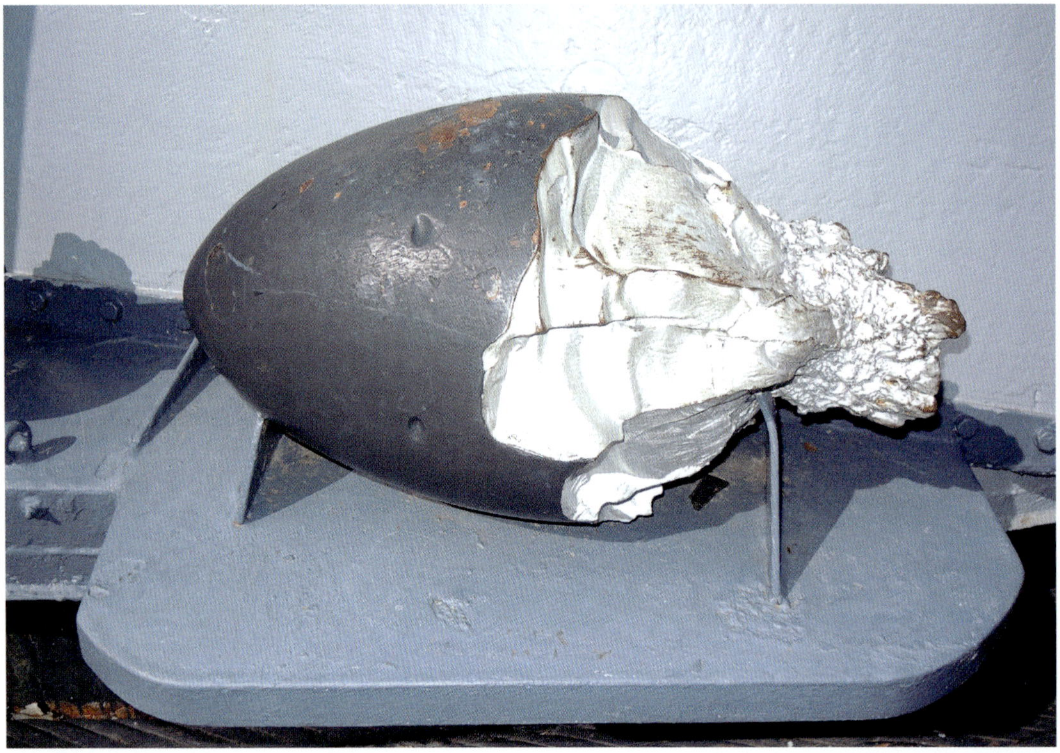

16-inch projectile fragment recovered from Casablanca battle area. (Christopher J. Nardi / USS *Massachusetts* Memorial Committee Inc.)

Damage to bulkheads of 5-inch Mount 9 and boat crane machinery room. This area is adjacent to the after quarterdeck. (Christopher J. Nardi / USS *Massachusetts* Memorial Committee Inc.)

(Photos by Edward Hayes)

World of Warships is a free-to-play, naval warfare–themed, massively multiplayer online game produced and published by Wargaming. Like their other games, *World of Tanks* (WoT) and *World of Warplanes* (WoWP), players take control of historic vehicles to battle others in player-versus-player or play ccooperatively against bots or in an advanced player-versus-environment (PvE) battle mode. *World of Warships* (WoWs) was originally released for PC in 2015; the PlayStation 4 and Xbox One console versions, titled *World of Warships: Legends*, followed in 2019, and it was released on the PlayStation 5 and Xbox Series X/S in April 2021.

Developed by Lesta Studios in St. Petersburg, Russia, *World of Warships* (PC) currently has more than 44 million registered players—playing on five main servers across the globe. More than 500 dedicated staff members work on a four-week update cycle to bring new features, ships, and mechanics to the game—keeping gameplay fresh and inviting to new players. The game features more than 400 ships, spread across 12 different in-game nations. Ships are designed based on historical documents and actual blueprints from the first half of the 20th century, and it takes from two to six man-months on average to create each of these ships. There are more than 20 ports to choose from, and 10 of them are re-created based on historical harbors and port towns.

There are four different ship classes: destroyers, cruisers, battleships, and aircraft carriers, with each class offering a different gameplay experience. Submarines have been in testing cycles since 2018, and based on testing results and player feedback, they have undergone significant changes that should allow them to launch as the fifth class in the near future. Ships are arranged in tiers between I and X, and players must progress through ship classes and tiers to reach tier X. Ships of tier X represent the pinnacle of naval engineering from World War II and the early Cold War era. Each warship needs a naval commander to lead it into the battle. There are many commanders to choose from in *World of Warships*, including more than 10 iconic historical figures. In *World of*